CHRISTUS VICTOR

CHRISTUS VICTOR

AN HISTORICAL STUDY OF
THE THREE MAIN TYPES
OF THE IDEA OF
ATONEMENT

by GUSTAF AULÉN

✧

TRANSLATED BY

A. G. HEBERT, M.A.

✧

Wipf & Stock
PUBLISHERS
Eugene, Oregon

Wipf and Stock Publishers
199 West 8th Avenue, Suite 3
Eugene, Oregon 97401

Christus Victor
An Historical Study of the Three Main Types of the Idea of Atonement
By Aulen, Gustaf
Copyright©1931 SPCK
ISBN: 1-59244-330-3
Publication date 9/5/2003
Previously published by SPCK, 1931

TABLE OF CONTENTS AND SUMMARY
OF THE ARGUMENT

1. The traditional account of the history of the idea of the Atonement envisages only the 'objective,' or Anselmian, and the 'subjective' or humanistic views.

2. But there is another type of view, commonly left almost out of sight; it may be summed up in two phrases—'Christus Victor,' and "God was in Christ reconciling the world to Himself." We shall see that this is the typical view of the New Testament and the Fathers, and was revived by Luther. We shall call this the 'classic' idea, and the Anselmian view the 'Latin.'

3. Four main reasons may be given why the classic idea has been neglected by the historians of dogma.

.4 Our thesis will require considerable modifications in the commonly accepted historical perspective, with regard to the early church and to Luther.

1. The purpose of the Incarnation, according to Irenæus, that God in Christ might deliver man from the enemies that hold him in bondage; sin, death, and the devil. The Recapitulation.

2. Sin and death are closely connected. Salvation is life; sin is a state of spiritual death, guiltiness, and separation from God. The devil represented as a usurper, and redemption as the restoration of God's original creation.

3. The redemptive work is carried out through the Incarnation of Christ, the Obedience of His human life, His Death and Resurrection, and the coming of the Spirit. Thereby God who reconciles is also reconciled, and Atonement is effected.

4. Conclusion.

PREFACE TO THE PAPERBACK EDITION

THE CENTRAL idea of *Christus Victor* is the view of God and the Kingdom of God as fighting against evil powers ravaging in mankind. In this drama Christ has the key rôle, and the title *Christus Victor* says the decisive word about his rôle. In the situation of theology today it may be, perhaps, even more needful to emphasize this perspective—the perspective of victory—than it was when my book first appeared.

Some critics have felt that the book underemphasized the importance of the humanity of Christ. I had no such intentions. His work cannot—as scholastic theology thought—be split into two parts, a divine and a human. It is a single unit, but a unit to be seen from two aspects: it is altogether a human work, and at the same time this human work is a divine work of creation and salvation.

Other critics, especially in continental Europe, thought that my treatment of what I called the "Latin" doctrine of the Atonement was too severe. My exposition, however, being a very short sketch, did not allow me to take into consideration the existence of modifications and variations which may be more valuable than the doctrine as a whole. Yet the decisive matter is obviously that the *structure* of this doctrine has a rationalizing character; in fact, it gives a rational explanation of the Atonement. This interpretation leads to fateful consequences as regards the image of God, and, indeed, the image of God is a main concern of my book. In this connection its aim is to expose three caricatures: the God of fatalism, where even the evil proceeds from God; the God

of moralism, where the spontaneity of the Love of God is
being killed; and finally the shallow view of God's Love,
where Love is considered self-evident, and where, therefore,
every sense of the Love's hard work has been lost. Concern-
ing gods of these types a "god-is-dead-theology" could do
us a service—especially if its death sentences were efficacious.
Then it would be a work in the service of the living God of
the Gospel.

GUSTAF AULÉN

Lund
 September, 1968

TRANSLATOR'S PREFACE

DR. AULÉN is Professor of Systematic Theology in the University of Lund, and this book is a translation of the Olaus Petri Lectures delivered by him before the University of Uppsala in March and April, 1930. The same lectures were also delivered in Germany in September, 1930, in a much condensed form, the eight lectures being brought down to three, with the title of *Die drei Haupttypen des christlichen Versöhnungsgedankens,* and were published in *Zeitschrift für systematische Theologie,* 1930, pp. 501–538.

This book is strictly an historical study; it contains no personal statement of belief or theory of the Atonement. Its important and original contribution is its strong delineation of the view of the Atonement which is summed up in such phrases as 'Christus Victor,' and 'God was in Christ reconciling the world to Himself'—the view that sets the Incarnation in direct connection with the Atonement, and proclaims that it is God Himself who in Christ has delivered mankind from the power of evil. As soon as the meaning of this view is grasped, the patristic teaching at once stands out as a strong, clear, and consistent whole, and it becomes impossible to doubt that it is this view which also dominates the New Testament; it has therefore every right to be called the typical Christian view, or, in Dr. Aulén's phrase, the 'classic' idea of the Atonement. Evidently, too, it is to be distinguished from the view which grew up in the West on the basis of the forensic idea of sin as transgression of law, and which received its first clear formulation from Anselm; for that view regards the Atonement as not in the full sense God's work, but rather as the act whereby man in Christ makes reparation for man's sin. Dr. Aulén proceeds to show that Luther revived the classic idea of the Atonement with mighty power, but that Luther's successors went back to the forensic view, which thus came to dominate orthodox Protestantism; and that the theologians of the 'subjective' or exemplarist view, which arose to challenge the accepted forensic theory, so far from returning to the classic idea, diverged from it still further, and concentrated their whole attention on the psychological process of man's reformation. Dr. Aulén closes with the hopeful expectation that we shall yet see the classic idea of the Atonement return in its strength; for with all his restraint, he cannot conceal where his own sympathies lie.

There will be many who will feel that this book sets out in black and white something that they have for a long time been feeling after. Many of us have been profoundly dissatisfied both with the satisfaction-theory and with the exemplarist explanations; we have had a dim sense that the 'classic' idea of the Atonement was there to be found, but we have not been able to get its true bearings, or to see what place it has actually held in the history of Christian thought. We have sought to give it tentative expression in sermons; and it is really significant that a Swedish Professor who paid a short visit to London in April, 1930, fresh from listening to Dr. Aulén at Uppsala, heard three different preachers on Good Friday and Easter Day, one of them a Congregationalist and two Anglo-Catholics, every one of whom preached on the Christus-victor theme.

To attempt to give anything like an adequate survey of the recent English literature on the Atonement would mean the addition of the equivalent of another chapter to this book. It may suffice to say that Dr. Rashdall's Bampton Lectures, *The*

Idea of the Atonement in Christian Theology, stand as one of the classical expressions of the 'subjective' view, while Dr. Kirk in *Essays Catholic and Critical* follows in all essentials the view of Anselm; and that, in spite of the prominence of the idea of the Incarnation in English theology, we have so far had only hesitating approaches towards the 'classic' idea of the Atonement. To this generalisation, however, there is at least one exception to be made: the great name of F. D. Maurice. But so influential a book as Moberly's *Atonement and Personality* is, in spite of its strongly orthodox tendency, almost nearer to the 'subjective' than to the 'classic' view; for its whole effort is directed to the discussion of man's return to God, and it never clearly seizes the theological basis of the 'classic' idea, that the redemption is, from first to last, the work of God Himself.

Here we may remark that the doctrine of the Incarnation is commonly treated, to a greater extent than is usually recognised, from a semi-Arian rather than from an Athanasian point of view. It is typical of semi-Arianism to define the Incarnation in such terms as that 'Jesus reveals God,' or 'God is like Jesus,' and to fail to see that the real question to be asked is 'What has God done?' The answer to this question leads at once and necessarily to the classic idea of the Atonement.

There are a number of ways in which recent theological work illustrates Dr. Aulén's main contention. First, we may notice the very decided turn which the exegesis of the Gospels is taking in the direction of finding the whole key to the problem of the Gospels in our Lord's belief in His Messiahship and the advent of the kingdom of God—in other words, in the Christology. Sir Edwyn Hoskyns' essay in *Mysterium Christi* is a sign of the times. The whole trend of this new exegesis is that the gospel message meant in the first place 'a movement of God to man,' and only secondarily a new ethical ideal.

Second, Dr. Aulén's sketch of the contrast between the patristic and mediæval views of the Atonement invites us to trace the same contrast in the sphere of liturgy; for the eucharistic rite is the liturgical representation of the Atonement. Dr. Brilioth, who is now Dr. Aulén's colleague at Lund, sets forth in his book *Eucharistic Faith and Practice, Evangelical and Catholic* (S.P.C.K., 1930), various aspects of the contrast between the rite of the early church, in which the communion of the people was a central feature, and the mediæval rite, in which there were only rarely any communicants besides the priest; and the change in sacramental practice corresponds closely to the change in the accepted idea of the Atonement. Similarly, Bishop Hicks, in *The Fullness of Sacrifice*, shows how the ancient and scriptural idea of sacrifice was displaced by the mediæval idea that sacrifice meant primarily immolation. Here, again, the narrowing of the idea of sacrifice might be shown to be closely connected with the changed idea of the Atonement. Once again, Dr. Herwegen, Abbot of Maria Laach, gives in two small pamphlets, *Kirche und Seele* and *Christliche Kunst und Mysterium*,[1] a valuable comparison between the religion of the early church period, which centred round the Christian Mystery—that is to say, both the Redemption and the Sacrament—and the religion of the Middle Ages, which to a large extent lost its hold on the sacramental principle, and by its predominantly individualistic and psychological interest prepared the way for the coming of modern subjectivism. He gives a variety of illustrations, of which perhaps the most interesting is the contrast between the catacomb paintings, which portray various aspects of the Mystery, and such work as Leonardo da Vinci's "Last Supper," where the whole interest is psychological and the institution of the sacrament drops clean out of sight.

[1] Published by Aschen Dorff, Münster-in-Westfalen, 1928 and 1929.

Third, there is the place which Dr. Aulén assigns to Luther; and this is perhaps the feature in the book which will most surprise the English reader. Some of us have been accustomed to view the figure of Luther with suspicion and dislike. Probably we have tended to interpret Luther in the light of the Lutheran Orthodoxy of the succeeding century. But Dr. Aulén shows how sharp is the contrast between Luther and the Lutherans.

This last reflection may help us to see fresh light on the greatest of all problems which confront Christendom to-day, the problem of Reunion. Luther spoke of the Babylonish Captivity of the sacrament and of the church. What was this captivity? And has the church's deliverance from captivity yet arrived?

Certainly, as this book shows, the Reformation was far more than a mere protest against abuses. It was an endeavour to deliver the Christendom of the West from the domination of a system, which had entangled the gospel of salvation in a rationalised theology and a moralistic ethic. Christianity had been turned into a system; man's way to God was interpreted as a way of justification by works and by human merit: the church had returned again under the yoke of bondage, from which St. Paul had told the Galatians that Christ had set them free. So Luther proclaimed; he believed with all his heart that God had given to him the message of deliverance. Perhaps in 1520 he also believed that God's hour of deliverance had come; if he did, it was not long before he was disillusioned, and we can well understand, from this point of view, the bitterness with which he flung abroad the accusation of "fanaticism." And Dr. Aulén shows how in regard to this central doctrine of redemption, Melanchthon led the people back into Egypt. The Protestant churches had not, after all, found the way of deliverance from the Babylonish Captivity; Protestant Orthodoxy was as legalistic as mediæval scholasticism, and Christendom was as hopelessly in bondage as before, and more hopelessly divided. In our day the great hope of Reunion has come; but the Reunion movement is confronted by the immense difficulty of reconciling the Catholic and the Protestant conceptions of faith and order.

But Dr. Aulén's interpretation of the history of the idea of the Atonement throws real light on the situation. He shows us that at this centrally important point, the New Testament, the early church, and Luther agree in taking the 'classic' view; while the rationalised theology of the satisfaction-doctrine belongs both to the Middle Ages which provoked the schism of the Reformation, and the post-Reformation period which has continued the schism; and the equally rationalistic 'subjective' theory appeared in both periods, and failed to provide a solution. In other words, the satisfaction-theory and the subjective doctrine both belong to the era of the church's 'captivity,' but the 'classic' view of redemption is at once truly evangelical and truly catholic.

Here, then, is the true hope of Reunion; not in the victory of 'Catholic' over 'Protestant,' or of 'Protestant' over 'Catholic,' but in the return of both to the rock whence they were hewn. There can be no true Reunion on the basis either of the Catholicism which delights to represent itself as the ideal religious system, or of the old Protestantism with its rigidity and its negations, or of the newer humanising, modernist Protestantism. Reunion is to come by the rediscovery of the old evangelical and catholic faith by all sections of Christendom in common; thus will come the escape from the perversions and narrowings of Christianity, of which all sections of Christendom have been guilty, to the gospel of God's redemption, and to the richness of a Catholicism which is truly evangelical. For the Jerusalem which is above is free, and is the mother of us all.

Dr. Aulén is perhaps the foremost dogmatic theologian of the Swedish Church, and his name is well known on the Continent, especially in Holland and Germany. He has written a number of other books, of which the most important are his work on the catholic (universal) Christian faith (*Den allmänneliga kristna tron*, Stockholm, 1923, now appearing in a third edition, 1931), and on the Christian idea of God (*Den kristna gudsbilden*, Stockholm, 1927). These lectures on the Atonement were published in 1930 by Svenska kyrkans diakonistyrelses bokförlag, under the title of *Den kristna försoningstanken* (The Christian Idea of the Atonement). The English title, *Christus Victor*, is therefore strictly a *pars pro toto;* the sub-title is taken from that of the German version of these lectures, to which reference has been made above.

This English version reproduces the whole of the matter of the original; a certain amount of shortening has, however, been necessary in order to reduce the lectures from an oral to a literary style. The work has been revised throughout by Dr. Aulén, and has received from him a few small additions.

A. G. HERBERT, s.s.m.

Kelham, Newark.
June, 1931.

1

THE PROBLEM AND ITS ANSWERS

MY WORK on the history of Christian doctrine has led me to an ever-deepening conviction that the traditional account of the history of the idea of the Atonement is in need of thorough revision. The subject has, indeed, received a large share of attention at the hands of theologians; yet it has been in many important respects seriously misinterpreted. It is in the hope of making some contribution to this urgently needed revision that this work has been undertaken.

I. THE TRADITIONAL ACCOUNT

Let us first take a rapid survey of the history of the idea of the Atonement, according to the generally accepted view.

The early church had, it is said, no developed doctrine of the Atonement, properly so called. The contributions of the patristic period to theology lie in another direction, being chiefly concerned with Christology and the doctrine of the Trinity; in regard to the Atonement, only hesitating efforts were made along a variety of lines, and the ideas which found expression were usually clothed in a fantastic mythological dress. The real beginnings of a thought-out doctrine of the Atonement are found in Anselm of Canterbury, who thus comes to hold a position of first-rate importance in the history of dogma. By the theory of satisfaction developed in the *Cur Deus homo?* he repressed, even if he could not entirely overcome, the old mythological account of Christ's work as a victory over the devil; in place of the older and more 'physical' idea of salvation he put forward his teaching of a deliverance from the guilt of sin; and, above all, he clearly taught an 'objective' Atonement, according to which God is the object of Christ's atoning work, and is reconciled through the satisfaction made to His justice. Needless to say, it is not implied that Anselm's teaching was wholly original. The stones lay ready to hand; but it was he who erected them into a monumental building.

A typical expression of the view which we have described is that of Ritschl, in *Die christliche Lehre von der Rechtfertigung und Versöhnung*. The very full historical section of this book begins with an introductory chapter on certain aspects of "the doctrine of salvation in the Greek church"; the use of the term *Erlösung*, salvation, indicates that, in his view, the history of the doctrine of the Atonement proper had not yet begun. This chapter is immediately followed by one entitled "The Idea of Atonement through Christ in Anselm and Abelard."

Typical again is the collocation of the names of Anselm and Abelard. These two are commonly contrasted as the authors respectively of the 'objective' and 'subjective' doctrines of the Atonement; the latter term is used to describe a doctrine which explains the Atonement as consisting essentially in a change taking place in men rather than a changed attitude on the part of God.

In the subsequent history of the doctrine, it is held that a continuous line may be traced from Anselm, through mediæval scholasticism, and through the Reformation, to the Protestant 'Orthodoxy' of the seventeenth century. It is not implied that the teaching of Anselm was merely repeated, for differences of view are noted in Thomas Aquinas and in the

Nominalists, and the post-Reformation statements of the doctrine have a character of their own; nevertheless, there is a continuity of tradition, and the basis of it is that which Anselm laid. It must specially be noted that the Reformation is included in this summary, and that it is treated as self evident that Luther had no special contribution to make, but followed in all essentials the Anselmian tradition. Those writers, however, who are opposed to that tradition readily allow an unsolved contradiction in Luther's world of ideas, between the mediæval doctrine of Atonement which he left unchanged, and the religious outlook which inspired his reforming work and his teaching of Justification by Faith.

Finally, according to the traditional account, the last two centuries have been marked by the coexistence of these two types, the 'objective' and the 'subjective,' and by the controversies between them. The subjective type has connections with Abelard, and with a few other movements here and there, such as Socinianism; but its rise to power came during the period of the Enlightenment. The nineteenth century is characterised by the conflict of this view with what was left of the 'objective' doctrine, as well as by a variety of compromises; Ritschl regards the period of the Enlightenment as that of the *Zersetzung* or disintegration of the 'objective' doctrine, and gives as a chapter heading "The Revival of the Abelardian type of Doctrine by Schleiermacher and his Disciples." Naturally, both sides found support for their respective views in the New Testament. Those who sought to uphold, with or without modifications, the tradition of Protestant Orthodoxy, contended vigorously for the 'biblical basis' of this type of Atonement-theory; the other side sought to show that the New Testament could not possibly be made to cover the teaching which was readily allowed the name of "the church doctrine." In this controversy the exegesis of Scripture suffered cruelly and long.

Such is the common account of the history of the doctrine of the Atonement. But we may well question whether it is satisfactory.

2. THE 'CLASSIC' IDEA OF THE ATONEMENT

There is a form of the idea of the Atonement which this account of the matter either ignores altogether or treats with very much less than justice, but whose suppression falsifies the whole perspective, and produces a version of the history which is seriously misleading. This type of view may be described provisionally as the 'dramatic.' Its central theme is the idea of the Atonement as a Divine conflict and victory; Christ—Christus Victor—fights against and triumphs over the evil powers of the world, the 'tyrants' under which mankind is in bondage and suffering, and in Him God reconciles the world to Himself. Two points here require to be pressed with special emphasis: first, that this is a doctrine of Atonement in the full and proper sense, and second, that this idea of the Atonement has a clear and distinct character of its own, quite different from the other two types.

First, then, it must not be taken for granted that this idea may rightly be called only a doctrine of salvation, in contrast with the later development of a doctrine of Atonement properly so called. Certainly it describes a work of salvation, a drama of salvation; but this salvation is at the same time an atonement in the full sense of the word, for it is a work wherein God reconciles the world to Himself, and is at the same time reconciled. The background of the idea is dualistic;[1] God is pictured as in Christ carrying through a victori-

---

[1] It will be well to explain at this point, once and for all, the sense in which the word Dualism is used in this book. It is not used in the sense of a metaphysical Dualism between the Infinite and the finite, or between spirit and matter; nor, again, in the sense of the absolute Dualism between Good and Evil typical of the Zoroastrian and Manichean teaching, in which Evil is treated as an eternal principle opposed

ous conflict against powers of evil which are hostile to His will. This constitutes Atonement, because the drama is a cosmic drama, and the victory over the hostile powers brings to pass a new relation, a relation of reconciliation, between God and the world; and, still more, because in a measure the hostile powers are regarded as in the service of the Will of God the Judge of all, and the executants of His judgment. Seen from this side, the triumph over the opposing powers is regarded as a reconciling of God Himself; He is reconciled by the very act in which He reconciles the world to Himself.

Secondly, it is to be affirmed that this 'dramatic' view of the Atonement is a special type, sharply distinct from both the other types. We shall illustrate its character fully in the course of these lectures; for the present a preliminary sketch must suffice.

The most marked difference between the 'dramatic' type and the so-called 'objective' type lies in the fact that it represents the work of Atonement or reconciliation as from first to last a work of God Himself, a *continuous* Divine work; while according to the other view, the act of Atonement has indeed its origin in God's will, but is, in its carrying-out, an offering made to God by Christ as man and on man's behalf, and may therefore be called a *discontinuous* Divine work.

On the other hand, it scarcely needs to be said that this

---

to Good. It is used in the sense in which the idea constantly occurs in Scripture, of the opposition between God and that which in His own created world resists His will; between the Divine Love and the rebellion of created wills against Him. This Dualism is an altogether radical opposition, but it is not an absolute Dualism; for in the scriptural view evil has not an eternal existence. We shall see later that in the dominant theology of the eighteenth and nineteenth centuries there has been a tendency to confuse this scriptural idea of Dualism with the other two forms, and therefore an effort to escape from it and to minimise its importance (see pp. 11, 54 f., 148 n.).

'dramatic' type stands in sharp contrast with the 'subjective' type of view. It does not set forth only or chiefly a change taking place in men; it describes a complete change in the situation, a change in the relation between God and the world, and a change also in God's own attitude. The idea is, indeed, thoroughly 'objective'; and its objectivity is further emphasised by the fact that the Atonement is not regarded as affecting men primarily as individuals, but is set forth as a drama of a world's salvation.

Since, then, the objective character of the 'dramatic' type is definite and emphatic, it can hardly help to a clear understanding of the history of the idea of Atonement to reserve the term 'objective Atonement' for the type of view which commonly bears that name. The result can only be a confusion of two views of the Atonement which need to be clearly distinguished. I shall therefore refer to the type of view commonly called objective as the 'Latin' type, because it arose and was developed on Western, Latin soil, and to the dualistic-dramatic view as 'the classic idea' of the Atonement.

The classic idea has in reality held a place in the history of Christian doctrine whose importance it would not be easy to exaggerate. Though it is expressed in a variety of forms, not all of which are equally fruitful, there can be no dispute that it is the dominant idea of the Atonement throughout the early church period. It is also in reality, as I shall hope to show, the dominant idea in the New Testament; for it did not suddenly spring into being in the early church, or arrive as an importation from some outside source. It was, in fact, the ruling idea of the Atonement for the first thousand years of Christian history. In the Middle Ages it was gradually ousted from its place in the theological teaching of the church, but it survived still in her devotional language and in her art. It confronts us again, more vigorously and profoundly expressed than ever before, in Martin Luther, and it constitutes an important part of his expression of the Christian faith. It has therefore every right to claim the title of the *classic Christian idea of the Atonement*. But if this be the case, any account of the history of the doctrine which does not give full consideration to this type of view cannot fail to be seriously misleading.

3. THE CAUSES OF THE NEGLECT OF THE CLASSIC IDEA OF THE ATONEMENT

It must be regarded as a problem requiring serious consideration, that a view of the Atonement which has in fact held so important a place in the history of doctrine should have received such scant consideration from modern theologians. The problem is far too complicated to be accounted for adequately in a few pages; but it is necessary to give the outline of an answer.

(i.) A first reason may be found in the controversial background of the theology of the eighteenth and nineteenth centuries; the historians of dogma were all engaged either in attacking or in defending the Protestant Orthodoxy of the seventeenth century. The historical study of dogma took its rise in the period of the Enlightenment. The theologians of the Enlightenment were the declared enemies of orthodoxy; and a chief object of their assault was just the satisfaction-theory of the Atonement, which they described as a relic of Judaism surviving in Christianity. So began the controversy between the 'objective' and the 'subjective' views of the Atonement, which continued through the nineteenth century, and was waged with extreme bitterness on both sides.

But the fact that the problem was stated in this way was scarcely likely to help towards a just view of the real history of the doctrine of the Atonement. The atmosphere was controversial; the shadow of Protestant Orthodoxy lay across the field of view; the whole of the earlier development of the doctrine was judged from the point of view of the controversy, and the disputants had little attention to spare for what lay outside its scope. Those who were engaged in the defence of Orthodoxy found the 'orthodox' ideas of the Atonement everywhere, even in Luther and in the New Testament; the other side sought as eagerly for points on which to hang their 'subjective' interpretation. Both sides lacked real freedom of judgment.

(ii.) Thus theologians have tended to confuse the classic idea of the Atonement with the Latin view. The patristic interpretations of the meaning of Christ's redemptive work have usually been treated as the first rude beginnings of the theory of the Atonement which was to receive its full and clear expression from Anselm of Canterbury. The recognition in both cases of an objective treatment of the subject led to the inference that there was no essential difference of view in either case. But if the Fathers of the early church give no more than the first rough draft of the theory which the scholastics of the Middle Ages brought to ripeness and perfection, it follows that their work has only a provisional and temporary importance. This is the explicit contention of the Roman Catholic theologian J. Rivière, in his book *Le dogme de la Rédemption,* and it is the usual view both of Roman theologians and of the Protestant historians of dogma in the nineteenth century.

This failure to distinguish clearly between the classic and Latin types of view is made easier by the fact that a whole series of ideas and images are employed in common by both; and wherever such terms as 'sacrifice' or 'substitution' occur, or analogies from legal procedure are employed, they are usually assumed to prove the presence of the 'objective' or 'juridical' view of the Atonement—in other words, the Latin type. But such conclusions are too hasty. In reality the closest attention needs to be given to the passages in which these phrases and images occur; for it does not by any means follow that the use of legal analogies implies that the writer has in his mind a Latin view of the Atonement. It can sometimes happen, and it actually happens in the case of Luther, that even the most characteristic terms of the Latin view, such as 'satisfaction' or 'the merits of Christ,' are detached from their usual connections, and used in a quite different meaning.

There is need, therefore, of the greatest caution in the exegesis of the language used of the Atonement. The meaning of the terms is not uniform. Phrases which had become stereotyped can alter their meaning. Above all, the greatest wariness is needed in the interpretation of phrases derived from Scripture before conclusions are drawn as to the idea of the Atonement present in a writer's mind.

(iii.) Neither the conservative theologians who defended the Orthodox theology, nor the 'liberal' theologians who attacked it, were naturally disposed to give sympathetic consideration of the classic idea of the Atonement. The conservative side tended to depreciate the dramatic view, as we have seen, because it had never attained to a clearly formulated theory; it was therefore regarded as representing a lower theological level, and as being able to contribute only images and symbolical expressions, not a clearly worked-out theological scheme. There lies behind this criticism a particular view of the nature of theology: an implied demand that the Christian faith must be clearly expressed in the form of a rational doctrine. It was felt, if it was not stated in so many words, that the superiority which Anselm was assumed to possess over the Fathers of the early church lay in the greater rationality of his teaching.

The theologians of the 'liberal' school were no less naturally inclined to be critical of the forms in which the patristic teaching had usually expressed itself. They disliked intensely

the 'mythological' language of the early church about
Christ's redemptive work, and the realistic, often undeniably
grotesque imagery, in which the victory of Christ over the
devil, or the deception of the devil, was depicted in lurid
colours. Thus the whole dramatic view was branded as
'mythological.' The matter was settled. The patristic teaching was of inferior value, and could be summarily relegated
to the nursery or the lumber-room of theology. There is no
difficulty in finding examples. H. Rashdall, who in his book
The Idea of Atonement in Christian Theology treats the
patristic teaching with relative fulness, finds repeated occasion to express his lively condemnation of the phraseology of
a transaction with the devil; such a theory is, he says, hide-
ous, and cannot be taken seriously. Similarly, A. E. N.
Hitchcock, in an article "A Modern Survey of the Atonement," in *The Modern Churchman* (Vol. xv., pp. 594 ff.),
distinguishes four main theories. Lowest of all he rates the
"ransom-theory" of the early church, whose leading idea is
that God saves mankind from the devil's power. This theory
he rejects as grotesque: "we can hardly imagine God 'doing
a deal' with Satan." The same general attitude can be plenti-
fully illustrated from Continental theologians. It may suffice
to recall some words of Ritschl, on the subject of the occurrence of the dramatic idea of the Atonement in Luther.
On Luther's language about the conflict of Christ with the
powers of evil he pronounces the judgment that "This is,
however, no improvement in comparison with mediæval
theology."[2] We know that his estimate of the Anselmian
satisfaction-theory, to which he here refers, was the lowest
possible.

The feature of all these criticisms is that the analysis made
by the historian of dogma goes no deeper than the outward

[2] Ritschl, *Rechtfertigung und Versöhnung*, I., p. 224.

dress. No serious attempt is made to penetrate behind the outward form to the underlying idea.

(iv.) There is also another and a deeper reason. Dualism[a] was not popular with the Liberal Protestant theology of the eighteenth and nineteenth centuries; but the classic idea of the Atonement is dualistic and dramatic: it depicts the drama of the Atonement against a dualistic background. If Dualism is eliminated, it is impossible to go on thinking of the existence of powers hostile to God, and the basis of the classic view has been dissolved away. Now, the leading theology from the time of the Enlightenment to the nineteenth century lay under the influence of an idealistic metaphysic, and was definitely monistic and evolutionary. It had no place for the dualistic element in Christianity; and this theological attitude reacted on its studies in the history of dogma in the New Testament and the patristic period.

Naturally, it was impossible for any historian to deny the presence of a dualistic element in primitive Christianity; but there was a predisposition to treat it as an accidental and non-essential phenomenon. The Enlightenment branded Dualism as demonological mythology, and explained its occurrence by the theory of an accommodation on the part of Jesus and His disciples to contemporary ways of thought. The nineteenth century was specially interested in investigating the historical origins of the dualistic idea along the lines of comparative religion, and finding traces of Zoroastrian influence.

Such historical studies have their own interest and importance. But in this case the historical study of origins was linked up with the question of the place and the meaning and value of the dualistic idea in Christianity; and the underlying assumption was that the dualistic outlook was to be

[a] See footnote to p. 4, above.

set on one side as irrelevant, since it was an element that had come in from outside into Judaism and primitive Christianity. That is to say, two questions were being brought together, which ought always to be kept strictly separate: the questions of origin and of value. The result was that the historical importance of the dualistic element in primitive Christianity came to be under-estimated; it was regarded as unessential, as an accidental addition. But in reality it is an integral and necessary element in primitive Christianity, and in the early church too. It is impossible to eliminate it without representing early Christianity as something quite other than it actually was.

It is equally important for us to avoid the same mistake ourselves; I desire, therefore, to guard against the imputation that I have been criticising the nineteenth-century theologians for the judgments of value which they pronounced on the classic idea of the Atonement. It is not the concern of scientific historical analysis to make or to criticise judgments of value. My aim is, therefore, simply to analyse the actual types of Atonement-doctrine, so that their characteristics may emerge with the greatest possible clearness, and to fix the actual development of these types in the course of Christian thought. My criticism of the nineteenth-century theologians is that the classic idea of the Atonement was not apprehended with sufficient clearness, nor due regard paid to its actual importance in the history of doctrine; and I have suggested certain causes which may help to explain this limitation of outlook.

4. THE HISTORICAL PERSPECTIVE

The subject of the Atonement is absolutely central in Christian theology; and it is directly related to that of the nature of God. Each and every interpretation of the Atonement is most closely connected with some conception of the

essential meaning of Christianity, and reflects some conception of the Divine nature. Indeed, it is in some conception
of the nature of God that every doctrine of the Atonement
has its ultimate ground. The history of the doctrine of the
Atonement is so important a part of the history of Christian
thought in general that the judgment which is formed on
this part of the history, on its conflicts and its changes, must
largely determine the judgment which is formed as to the
meanings of Christian history in general. It is evident, therefore, that the thesis which we are maintaining raises some
very wide issues.

If the view of the history maintained in this book can be
substantiated, it will necessitate a very different view of the
patristic period, both in itself and in its relation to the New
Testament, from that which was presented by the nineteenth-century historians of dogma. It seems to me entirely
probable that the next few years will see a thorough revision
of the interpretation of the early church which found a
monumental expression in Harnack's great *History of
Dogma.* Our interpretation of Luther has undergone a complete revision in the last thirty years; the turn of the patristic
period will come next. If I am not altogether mistaken, it
will become evident that the interpretation of the Christology of the period as "a work of the Hellenistic spirit,"
intellectualistic and metaphysical in character, and of its
doctrine of salvation as 'naturalistic,' rests rather on the pre-
suppositions of nineteenth-century theology than on an objective and unprejudiced analysis of the actual work of the
Fathers. If the patristic view of the Atonement has really
the character which we have attributed to it, it will become
impossible to maintain the common view of its Christology
as merely metaphysical and its doctrine of salvation as naturalistic. We have further suggested that there is in reality a
close relation between the Fathers and the New Testament,

and an essential difference between them and the Latin type of thought which gradually grew to its full development in the mediæval scholastics.

Again, Luther's handling of the doctrine of the Atonement throws an important light on his place in the general history of Christian doctrine. If it is true that Luther's doctrine of Christ's redemptive work coheres in all essentials with the early church view, it follows that he stands in sharp opposition to the typically Latin view. Obviously, the breach which Luther made with the Latin type of Christianity cannot be regarded as fundamental so long as it is assumed that Luther's teaching on the Atonement is of a piece with that of the mediæval, Anselmian tradition, and that a violent opposition exists between his Atonement-doctrine and his teaching of Justification by Faith. But now Luther's outlook becomes far more harmonious; it becomes far clearer than before that, not only at certain isolated points, but along the whole line, Luther challenged the Latin interpretation of Christianity.

At the same time it becomes possible to look for new connections between Luther and the earlier forms of the classic tradition, both in the New Testament and in the early ɪch. It now becomes more impossible than ever to treat the Reformation as a revolt against the Catholic Church of Christ. The claim of the evangelical Confessions, especially the Augsburg Confession, to represent an evangelical catholicism had in reality a firmer foundation of truth than the Reformers themselves understood.

If our hypothesis is true, the Latin type of Christian doctrine turns out to be really a side-track in the history of Christian dogma—admittedly of vast importance and influence, but still only a side-track; and the proud claim of Roman theology to represent the continuity of Christian doctrine cannot be substantiated. The history of the doctrine of the Atonement shows clearly that just at this central point the Latin view definitely deviates from the classic Christian view. The main line in the development of doctrine is continued, not by Anselm and the mediæval scholastics, but by Luther.

2

IRENÆUS

WE HAVE now to undertake a survey, in broadest outline, of the history of the doctrine of the Atonement. We take for our starting-point the teaching of the Fathers, and begin with a study, in some detail, of Irenæus, the earliest Father to give a thorough treatment of the subject.

This method of procedure may seem surprising; but it has much to commend it. Every interpretation of the Atonement goes back to the New Testament texts, and seeks to base itself upon them; it is difficult, therefore, to read those texts without associating them with some pre-conceived theory. On the other hand, the teaching of Irenæus, a hundred years later, is quite clear and its meaning indisputable; there is, then, an obvious advantage in beginning at this point. The teaching of the early Fathers is bound to throw an important light on the teaching of the Apostolic age itself; and in general it may be remarked that it is often useful to read history backwards, and see how the subsequent development of thought illuminates the preceding stages.

The choice of Irenæus as our starting-point among the Fathers is amply justifiable on general grounds. It is true that we do not find in him the brilliant style of Tertullian, the philosophical erudition of Clement or Origen, or the religious depth of Augustine. Yet of all the Fathers there is not one who is more thoroughly representative and typical, or who did more to fix the lines on which Christian thought was to move for centuries after his day. His strength lies in the fact that he did not, like the Apologists and the Alexandrians, work along some philosophical line of approach to Christianity, but devoted himself altogether to the simple exposition of the central ideas of the Christian faith itself. Thus Bousset writes of him that he is *the* theologian who sets forth, more clearly than any of his contemporaries or immediate successors, "the future form of things";[1] that he is unexcelled in the richness and manifoldness of the ideas which he gathers up and expresses in simple and adequate formulations; and that in this respect he may be called the Schleiermacher of the second century. Our choice of Irenæus may, then, be justified on the ground of his general theological importance, as well as of the undoubted fact that he is the first patristic writer to provide us with a clear and comprehensive doctrine of the Atonement and redemption. The smaller writings of the Apostolic Fathers treat of this theme in a relatively incidental way, and the same is true of the extant works of the Apologists; though this does not at all imply that the subject itself was in any way of secondary importance for those writers. But with Irenæus it is otherwise. The idea of the Atonement recurs continually in his writings, freshly treated from ever new points of view; his basic idea is in itself thoroughly clear and unmistakable, and also, as we shall see in the next chapter, marks out the track which succeeding generations were to follow. We may, then, feel satisfied that we have found in Irenæus our true starting-point.

[1] "Die künftige Gestaltung der Dinge," *Kyrios Christos,* 3rd edn., p. 334.

I. THE PURPOSE OF THE INCARNATION

Ut quid enim descendebat?[2] asks Irenæus. For what purpose did Christ come down from heaven? The answer which he gives to this question will be the key to his whole theology.

Passages from Irenæus are commonly quoted in this sense: Christ became man that we might be made divine; "we could not otherwise attain to incorruption and immortality except we had been united with incorruption and immortality."[3] Without doubt these words contain an important side of his teaching; but the matter demands closer investigation.

Irenæus has been commonly interpreted by theologians of the Liberal Protestant school as teaching a 'naturalistic' or 'physical' doctrine of salvation; salvation is the bestowal of 'divinity'—that is, of immortality—on human nature, and the idea of deliverance from sin occupies quite a secondary place.[4] The gift of immortality is regarded as dependent on the Incarnation as such; by the entrance of the Divine into humanity, human nature is (as it were) automatically endued with Divine virtue and thereby saved from corruption. This is, then, a theology primarily of the Incarnation, not of the Atonement; the 'work' of Christ holds a secondary place. So Harnack interprets Irenæus: "The work of Christ is contained in the construction of His person as the God-man."[5] Anglo-Catholic writers have not infrequently accepted and upheld a somewhat similar view of the Incarnation, in conscious opposition to the pietistic-orthodox doctrine of the

---

[2] *Adv. Hæreses*, II., 14. 7. For the quotations from Irenæus Harvey's text has been followed.

[3] *Adv. Hær.*, IV., 33. 4. *Cf.* "Quomodo enim homo transiet in Deum, si non Deus in hominem?" (III., 19. 1).

[4] *Cf.* Harnack, *History of Dogma*, E.T. II., 274.

[5] *Ibid.*, p. 293.

Atonement which is characteristic of the Evangelical school, and have justified this rival emphasis on the Incarnation by the appeal to the Fathers.

It is true that such an opposition of the Atonement and the Incarnation would be intelligible enough if the only possible view of the Atonement were that of the Latin type; for, as we shall see later on, the Latin doctrine always involves an opposition, expressed or implied, between the Incarnation and the work of Christ. But the opposition becomes meaningless as soon as the 'classic' idea of the Atonement receives due consideration; for in this type of view the Incarnation and the Atonement always stand in the closest relation to one another. And other passages of Irenæus show that the interpretation to which we refer seriously misrepresents his meaning.

Let us, then, put the question again: For what purpose did Christ come down from heaven? Answer: "That He might destroy sin, overcome death, and give life to man."* By the side of this pregnant saying we will set another, chosen from among many similar passages, which develops the dramatic idea in fuller detail: "Man had been created by God that he might have life. If now, having lost life, and having been harmed by the serpent, he were not to return to life, but were to be wholly abandoned to death, then God would have been defeated, and the malice of the serpent would have overcome God's will. But since God is both invincible and magnanimous, He showed His magnanimity in correcting man, and in proving all men, as we have said; but through the Second Man He bound the strong one, and spoiled his goods, and annihilated death, bringing life to man who had become subject to death. For Adam had become the devil's possession, and the devil held him under his power, by hav-

* "Ut occideret quidem peccatum, evacuaret autem mortem, et vivificaret hominem" (*Adv. Hær.*, III., 18. 7).

ing wrongfully practised deceit upon him, and by the offer of immortality made him subject to death. For by promising that they should be as gods, which did not lie in his power, he worked death in them. Wherefore he who had taken man captive was himself taken captive by God, and man who had been taken captive was set free from the bondage of condemnation."[7]

In the first of these passages Irenæus speaks of sin and death as the enemies of mankind; in the second there emerges by the side of or behind death the figure of the devil. The main idea is clear. The work of Christ is first and foremost a victory over the powers which hold mankind in bondage: sin, death, and the devil. These may be said to be in a measure personified, but in any case they are objective powers; and the victory of Christ creates a new situation, bringing their rule to an end, and setting men free from their dominion.

What, then, is the place of the Incarnation in relation to the work of Christ and to His victory? It is indeed true, and it is of fundamental importance, that the Incarnation is the corner-stone of Irenæus' theology. But it is no more true to say that all depends on the Incarnation apart from the redemptive work than it would be to make all depend on the work apart from the Incarnation. To make an opposition between the two is altogether to miss the point. In Irenæus' thought, the Incarnation is the necessary preliminary to the atoning work, because only God is able to overcome the powers which hold man in bondage, and man is helpless. The work of man's deliverance is accomplished by God Himself, in Christ. This is the nerve of the whole conception. "The Word of God," he says, "was made flesh in order that He might destroy death and bring man to life; for we were

---

[7] *Adv. Hær.*, III., 23. 1.

tied and bound in sin, we were born in sin and live under the dominion of death."[8]

Thus the answer which Irenæus gives to the question *Cur Deus homo?* is simple and transparently clear; there is no trace of the cleavage between Incarnation and Atonement which appears in Anselm. Naturally, therefore, we find him avoiding every such form of expression as would tend to make a separation between the Father and the Son, by treating Christ as some sort of intermediary being. So, for instance, the Apologists sometimes speak of Him as δεύτερος Θεός, a second God; and a tendency to use such phrases creeps in wherever the doctrine of the Logos is interpreted in the light of contemporary Greek philosophy. But the attitude of Irenæus—who here represents the main line of patristic thought—expresses a determined opposition to this philosophical influence, just because the point of crucial importance with him is that it is God Himself, and not any intermediary, who in Christ accomplishes the work of redemption, and overcomes sin, death, and the devil. When he uses the term Logos, it is in the Johannine sense: "the Word is God Himself";[9] he never interprets the Logos as a Being separate from God, and he uses the term with a characteristic reserve, preferring as a rule to use the term Son. It is his constant teaching that God Himself has entered into this world of sin and death: "the same hand of God that formed us in the beginning, and forms us in our mother's womb, in these latter days sought us when we were lost, gaining His lost sheep and laying it on His shoulders and bringing it back with joy to the flock of life."[10]

The Divine victory accomplished in Christ stands in the centre of Irenæus' thought, and forms the central element in the *recapitulatio*, the restoring and the perfecting of the

[8] *Epideixis* 37.   [9] "Verbum ipse Deus" (*Adv. Hær.*, II., 13).
[10] *Ibid.*, V., 15. 2.

creation, which is his most comprehensive theological idea.
The Recapitulation does not end with the triumph of Christ
over the enemies which had held man in bondage; it continues in the work of the Spirit in the church. At this point
Irenæus' language is far from bearing out the imputation
that his doctrine is 'naturalistic.' "They that fear God, and
believe in the advent of His Son, and by faith establish in
their hearts the Spirit of God, such are justly called men,
and spiritual, and alive unto God, who have the Spirit of the
Father, who cleanses man and exalts him to the life of God."[11]
But the completeness of the Recapitulation is not realised in
this life: Irenæus' outlook is strongly eschatological, and the
gift of the Spirit in this life is for him the earnest of future
glory. It remains true, however, that in the process of the
restoring and perfecting of creation—for both are involved
—the central and the crucial point is the victory of Christ
over the hostile powers. It is to these that we must next
direct our attention.

2. SIN, DEATH, AND THE DEVIL

First, we must ask in what relation the conceptions of sin
and death stand to one another in Irenæus. We have already
noted the assertion that he, in common with other Eastern
theologians, places relatively little emphasis on sin, because
he regards salvation as a bestowal of life rather than of forgiveness, and as a victory over mortality rather than over sin.

I shall hope to show that this assertion is quite misleading.
To begin with, I should like to quote some words from the
admirable little book of the Bulgarian theologian Stephen
Zankow on the Eastern Church,[12] words which, though writ-

---

11 *Adv. Hær.*, V., 9. 2.
12 *Das orthodoxe Christentum des Ostens.* Quotation from the English
translation, *The Orthodox Eastern Church*, by Donald A. Lowrie (London, 1929), pp. 49–50.

ten primarily with reference to the Eastern Church in general, are thoroughly applicable to Irenæus:

"Salvation from what? From sin or from death? Western theologians like to put this contrast, and claim that the Orthodox put death in the foreground instead of sin. But this is scarcely true. Orthodoxy is quite inclined, it is true, to conceive of original sin as the result of the first sin, and death as the reward of sins; yet, as has been said, empirically one is not separated from the other; where sin is, there is death also, and *vice versa.* . . . To the Orthodox the question 'Why salvation?' is very clear: in order to be free from sin and death, in order to break down the wall of partition between God and men, to enter into inner and complete communion with God, to be at one with Him."

Zankow mentions the names of Athanasius and Chrysostom, besides a number of more recent theologians; he might equally have mentioned Irenæus, for this close association of sin and death is specially characteristic of him. But if this is so, there can be no essential opposition between the two in his teaching, nor can he have thought of the evil of sin as of secondary importance.

This may be illustrated by a double contrast. First, Irenæus is definitely opposed to a moralistic view, which would have no other meaning for sin than as separate and individual acts of sin; on the contrary, he always regards sin organically. Second, here as elsewhere he is openly at issue with the Gnostic teaching which found the seat of sin in matter and in the body, and thus divided human nature into two parts—a lower self which is full of sin, and a higher, spiritual self. He thinks of sin as affecting the whole man. It is from one point of view an objective power, under which men are in bondage, and are not able to set themselves free; but from another point of view it is something voluntary and wilful, which makes men debtors in relation to God. "They who have fallen away from the Father's light, and transgressed the law of liberty, have fallen away through their own fault, for they were made free and self-determining. . . . Submission to God is eternal rest; so that they who fly from the light have such a place of flight as they deserve, and they who fly from eternal rest reach such a dwelling-place as befits their flight. But since all good is to be enjoyed in God, they who of their own choice fly from God defraud themselves of all good things."[13]

Mankind is thus guilty in God's sight, and has lost fellowship with God. Men were "by nature sons of God, because they were created by Him, but according to their deeds they are not His sons. For as among men disobedient sons, disowned by their parents, are indeed sons according to nature, but in law have become alienated, since they are no longer the heirs of their natural parents, so with God, they who do not obey Him are disowned by Him and cease to be His sons."[14] There is, then, enmity between mankind and God, an enmity which can only be taken away through an Atonement, a *reconciliatio*.[15] The enmity, which was expressed on God's side in the punishment of corruption which rested upon men, is now abolished by God Himself. He "had pity on men, and flung back on the author of enmities the enmity by which he had purposed to make man an enemy to God; He took away His enmity against men, and flung it back and cast it upon the serpent. So the Scripture says: I will put enmity between thee and the serpent, and between thy seed and the seed of the woman; he shall bruise thy head, and thou shalt watch for his heel. This enmity the Lord recapitulated in Himself, being made man, born of a woman, and bruising the serpent's head."[16]

We see now how it is that in Irenæus' thought sin and

---

[13] *Adv. Hær.*, IV., 39. 3.   [14] *Ibid.*, IV., 41. 2, 3.
[15] *Ibid.*, V., 14. 3.   [16] *Ibid.*, IV., 40. 3.

death are inseparably associated. Sin involves death; but it is also, as Bonwetsch is fully justified in saying, "a component part of death."[17] It is not merely that death is mortality and the loss of immortality; disobedience to God *is* essentially death. "Fellowship with God is life and light, and the fruition of the good things that are with Him. But on those who voluntarily rebel against God, He brings separation from Him; and separation from God is death."[18] It is passages such as this which explain the association of sin and death in Irenæus, and his use of the two terms to some extent interchangeably; when he speaks of salvation from death, his thought includes the idea of salvation from a state of sin. We have also here the explanation of his constant emphasis on salvation as a bestowal of Life. Life means for him primarily fellowship with God, the partaking of the life of God, and therefore also a deliverance from sin.

It is, then, wholly false to assume that in Irenæus the idea of sin is thrown into the background by a naturalistic conception of salvation. The truth is rather that Irenæus' organic view of sin as a state of alienation from God saves him both from a moralistic idea of sin and a moralistic idea of salvation. We may further remind ourselves that in all this he is in no way original; the ideas which we have been considering had already found full and clear expression in the New Testament, particularly in the Pauline and Johannine epistles, where we find the most definite statements that salvation is life, in direct connection with the thought of Christ as victor over sin and over death. In fact, the teaching that salvation is the bestowal of life holds the secret of the note of triumph which is characteristic of Apostolic Christianity.

By the side of Sin and Death Irenæus ranges the devil. But the phrase 'by the side of' scarcely does justice to his

---

17 "Ein Bestandtheil des Todes," *Die Theologie des Irenäus*, pp. 80 f.
18 *Adv. Hær.*, V., 27. 2.

thought; it is rather that, like later Eastern theologians, he passes insensibly from the one to the other. Yet at the same time it is certainly true that he thinks of the devil as having in some sense an objective existence, independent of sin and death. He is the lord of sin and death; he deceived mankind; and as men have followed him, they have fallen under his power, so that they may even be called his sons. "Those who do not believe in God, and do not do His will, are called sons, or angels, of the devil, since they do the works of the devil."[19] From the devil's dominion men cannot escape, except through the victory of Christ; and this victory is specially a triumph over the devil, for the devil is regarded as summing up in himself the power of evil, as he who leads men into sin and has the power of death. In a passage which describes the devil as a rebel and a robber, Irenæus says: "The Word of God, who is the creator of all things, overcame him through man, and branded him as an apostate, and made him subject to man. See, says the Word, I give you power to tread upon serpents and scorpions, and upon all the power of the enemy."[20]

But though the thought of the victory of Christ over the devil occurs very frequently in Irenæus, it is not so dominant a theme with him as with some of the later Greek Fathers, and it is not elaborated with anything like the same wealth of imagery. In particular, the realistic imagery which became exceedingly common later on is almost absent from Irenæus; there is only a trace in him of the theme of the Deception of the devil, which became to some of the other Fathers a subject of engrossing interest.

There is, however, one point that demands closer attention: the place which Irenæus finds for the element of justice in Christ's victory over the devil. The following is a characteristic passage: "He who is the almighty Word, and true

20 Ibid., V., 24. 4.   19 Adv. Hær., IV., 41. 2.

man, in redeeming us reasonably (*rationabiliter*) by His blood, gave Himself as the ransom for those who had been carried into captivity. And though the apostasy had gained its dominion over us unjustly, and, when we belonged by nature to almighty God, had snatched us away contrary to nature and made us its own disciples, the Word of God, who is mighty in all things, and in nowise lacking in the justice which is His, behaved with justice even towards the apostasy itself; and He redeemed that which was His own, not by violence (as the apostasy had by violence gained dominion over us at the first, insatiably snatching that which was not its own), but by persuasion (*secundum suadelam*), as it was fitting for God to gain His purpose by persuasion and not by use of violence; that so the ancient creation of God might be saved from perishing, without any infringement of justice."[21]

The statement which is sometimes made, that Irenæus is here propounding a 'juridical' doctrine of the Atonement, shows a complete misconception of his meaning. The real point is rather to be expressed as follows. Irenæus has two different ways of expressing the righteousness of God's act of redemption. According to the first, the devil cannot be allowed to have any rights over men; he is a robber, a rebel, a tyrant, a usurper, unjustly laying hands on that which does not belong to him. Therefore it is no more than justice that he should be defeated and driven out. The constant emphasis of Irenæus on this point is explained by his controversy with Marcion and the Gnostics; in opposition to the doctrine of the creation of the world by the Demiurge, he is jealous to insist that by the fact of his creation man belonged from the beginning to the true God, and that the God of redemption is also the God of creation.

But at the same time Irenæus also exhibits the righteousness of God's redemptive work, by showing that in it He does

[21] *Adv. Hær.*, V., 1. 1.

not use mere external compulsion, mere brute force, but acts altogether according to justice. "God deals according to justice even with the apostasy itself." For man after all is guilty; man has sold himself to the devil. Behind the somewhat obscure language about 'persuasion' (*secundum suadelam*) lies the thought that Christ gave Himself as a ransom paid to the devil for man's deliverance. Irenæus shrinks from the assertion which some of the later Fathers are prepared to make, that the devil has gained, in the last resort, certain actual rights over man; he is restrained by his sense of the importance of maintaining, against the Gnostics, that the devil is a robber and a usurper. Yet the underlying idea is present: the "apostasy" of mankind involves guilt, and man deserves to lie under the devil's power. In his reply he goes no further than to say that God acts in the way "that befits God"; even with the devil God deals in an orderly way. To call this a juridical doctrine of the Atonement is nonsense. Irenæus' real meaning would be more truly expressed by saying that God observes "the rules of fair play."

3. THE ATONING WORK

We must next ask how Irenæus sets forth the actual accomplishment of the work of atonement, and what special features he emphasises in his portrayal of Christ. We shall see that he traces a continuous line from the Incarnation, through the entire earthly life of Christ, and His death, to His resurrection and exaltation, and that no one point in this line claims anything like an exclusive emphasis.

We have already dealt with the contention that he lays the whole weight on the bare idea of the Incarnation; we have seen that, on the contrary, the Incarnation is essentially the indispensable basis on which the subsequent work of redemption rests. If he can sometimes speak of salvation as bestowed through the coming of Christ in the flesh, it is evident that he has no idea of playing off the Incarnation against the redemptive work; he is simply using a *pars pro toto*, including in the Incarnation all that to which it led up. The contention of Bonwetsch[22] that the Cross, and with it the Resurrection, holds no central place in Irenæus' thought, would be true enough in the sense that no exclusive emphasis is laid by him on the Cross; but in fact Bonwetsch's meaning seems to be that Irenæus treats the death of Christ as of quite secondary importance. As against this, Brunner is fully justified in claiming, in his excellent study of Irenæus in *Der Mittler*,[23] that the death of Christ has essentially the same significance for Irenæus as for Paul. But he too seems to be guilty of a shortening of the perspective, since the line which he draws stops short at the death. In truth, the emphasis which Irenæus lays on the triumph of Christ through conflict, and his interpretation of salvation as life, leads by an inner necessity to a stress on the Resurrection and Ascension.

Irenæus is altogether free from the tendency, which has shown itself at times in later theology, to emphasise the death of Christ in such a way as to leave almost out of sight the rest of His earthly life. It is remarkable what great weight he attaches to the Obedience of Christ throughout His life on earth. He shows how the disobedience of the one man, which inaugurated the reign of sin, is answered by the One Man who brought life. By His obedience Christ 're-capitulated' and annulled the disobedience.[24] The obedience is the means of His triumph: "By His obedience unto death the Word annulled the ancient disobedience committed at the tree."[25] This victorious obedience is specially seen in the

---

22 *Op. cit.*, p. 113.
23 P. 229. This book contains a vigorous criticism of Harnack, which is for the most part sound, but is not always fully justified.
24 *Adv. Hær.*, III., 21. 10; 22. 4.   25 *Epideixis* 34.

Temptations. But also His preaching and teaching are expressly regarded in the same light; the teaching by which we "learn to know the Father" forms an element in Christ's victory over the powers of darkness. Need it be added that it is beside the point to make this an excuse for reproaching Irenæus with 'intellectualism'?

But if the earthly life of Christ as a whole is thus regarded as a continuous process of victorious conflict, it is His death that is the final and decisive battle.[26] Naturally, Irenæus employs a whole series of biblical images. Here and there he uses the formula that Christ has redeemed us "by His blood"; but he has a special liking for the image of ransom, to which we have already alluded. The ransom is always regarded as paid to the powers of evil, to death, or to the devil; by its means they are overcome, and their power over men is brought to an end. It cannot be too strongly emphasised that when this has been done, atonement has taken place; for a new relation between God and the world is established by the fact that God has delivered mankind from the powers of evil, and reconciled the world to Himself. At this central point, God is both the Reconciler and the Reconciled. It is

[26] There is, indeed, in Irenæus no depreciation of the significance of Christ's death; and the remarks of Seeberg (*Lehrbuch der Dogmengeschichte*, 2nd edn., I., p. 330) fall into the mistake of reading Irenæus in the light of the Latin doctrine of the Atonement. Seeberg says: "The cross of Christ has not (in Irenæus) the significance which, after Paul, was usual. The death of Christ is indeed regarded as necessary, on account of the recapitulation; but the forgiveness of sins has not its basis in this, but appears as a function exercised by Christ in virtue of His Deity." He refers to *Adv. Hær.*, V., 17. 2, where Irenæus says: "Thus, in forgiving sins, He made men whole, and showed clearly who He was." Seeberg's argument shows a complete incapacity to understand the thought of Irenæus, and the nature of the classic idea of the Atonement. It may be remarked that it has always been something of a problem for the Latin theory how Christ could forgive sins in the days of His ministry. The classic idea finds, of course, no difficulty here; but this does not in the least involve any depreciation of the significance of the death on the cross.

God who, as active, accomplishes the work of salvation; but at the same time He is also, as passive, reconciled, because the bondage of helplessness under the powers of evil, from which He delivers man, is also, from another point of view, an enmity involving man's guilt.

This double-sidedness, of Divine activity and passivity, appears again when Irenæus uses the analogy of sacrifice to interpret the work of Christ. The sacrifice of Christ has relation both to God and to the powers of evil. On the one side "by His passion Christ has reconciled us to God";[27] on the other, it is God Himself who makes the sacrifice. "Abraham in faith followed the command of the word of God, and with a ready mind gave up his only-begotten son as a sacrifice to God; that it might also be the good pleasure of God, on behalf of all his seed, to give up His beloved and only-begotten Son as a sacrifice for our redemption."[28] Here the thought of sacrifice passes immediately to that of ransom. But the attribution to God alternately of activity and of passivity shows how very far we are in Irenæus from the rational theory of the Atonement which took shape as the Latin doctrine. It corresponds in fact to the double-sidedness of the Pauline formula: "God was in Christ, reconciling the world to Himself."[29]

Assuredly, then, the death of Christ holds a central place in Irenæus' thought. But, we must add at once, it is not the death in isolation; it is the death seen in connection, on the one hand, with the life-work of Christ as a whole, and on the other with the Resurrection and the Ascension; the death irradiated with the light of Easter and Pentecost.[30] The

---

[27] "Per passionem reconciliavit nos Deo" (*Adv. Hær.*, III., 16. 9).
[28] *Adv. Hær.*, IV., 5. 4. [29] 2 Cor. v. 19.
[30] Some words of Zankow (*op. cit.*, p. 55) are as true of Irenæus, and of the later Greek Fathers, as of Eastern Christianity in general: "Christ's Resurrection is inseparably connected with His death on the cross. For the Orthodox Church, as well for its theology as for its popu-

whole order of his thought, his whole emphasis on the victory of life, makes it clear that he cannot rest till he has
brought us to the thought of Christ as the Lord of Life. The
Resurrection is for him first of all the manifestation of the
decisive victory over the powers of evil, which was won on
the cross; it is also the starting-point for the new dispensation, for the gift of the Spirit, for the continuation of the
work of God in the souls of men "for the unity and communion of God and man."[31] "The passion of Christ brought
us courage and power. The Lord through His passion as-
cended up on high, led captivity captive, and gave gifts to
men, and gave power to them that believe in Him to tread
upon serpents and scorpions and upon all the power of the
enemy—that is, the prince of the apostasy. The Lord through
His passion destroyed death, brought error to an end, abolished corruption, banished ignorance, manifested life, declared truth, and bestowed incorruption."[32]

Irenæus' whole line of thought thus stands out in harmonious clearness. The Word of God, who is God Himself,
has entered in under the conditions of sin and death, to take
up the conflict with the powers of evil and carry it through
to the decisive victory. This has brought to pass a new relation between God and the world; atonement has been
made. The mercy of God has delivered men from the doom
which rested upon them. Thus a clear and simple answer
has been given to the question *Ad quid descendebat?* Christ
came down from heaven because no power other than that
of God Himself was able to accomplish the work that was
to be done. Incarnation and atoning work are thus set in the

---

lar conceptions, salvation is only finally complete in the Resurrection.
Sin and death are conquered, and life is bestowed upon men. Only the
Resurrection is the real earnest of salvation and of eternal life."

[31] "In adunitionem et communionem Dei et hominis" (*Adv. Hær.*, V.,
1. 1).   [32] *Adv. Hær.*, II., 20. 3.

closest possible relation to one another; both belong to one scheme.

There is yet one point that requires further comment, particularly in view of its importance in the subsequent history of the doctrine of the Atonement. The work of redemption is accomplished by Christ as man; might it not, then, seem that we have in Irenæus the same teaching which is specially characteristic of the Latin doctrine of the Atonement—namely, that Christ as man, from man's side, makes an acceptable offering to God? It might be possible to quote passages such as the following: "If man had not defeated the enemy of man, the enemy would not have been fairly (*juste*) overcome. Again, if God had not bestowed salvation, we should not possess it securely. And if man had not been united with God, he would not have been able to become partaker of immortality. For the mediator between God and man must through His relation to both bring both together into friendship and concord, that He might both present man to God, and that man might learn to know God."[33]

To read Irenæus in the light of the Latin theory is, however, to miss the essential distinction. He does not think of the Atonement as an offering made to God by Christ from man's side, or as it were from below; for God remains throughout the effective agent in the work of redemption. "The Word of God, who is the creator of all, overcoming him (the devil) through man (*per hominem vincens eum*), and declaring him an apostate, made him subject to man."[34] The redemptive work is accomplished *by* the Logos *through* the Manhood as His instrument; for it could be accomplished by no power but that of God Himself. When Irenæus speaks in this connection of the 'obedience' of Christ, he has no thought of a human offering made to God from man's side, but rather that the Divine will wholly dominated the

[33] *Ibid.*, III., 18. 6. [34] *Adv. Hær.*, V., 24. 4.

human life of the Word of God, and found perfect expression in His work.

4. CONCLUSION

The teaching of Irenæus is clear and consistent, and forms a thoroughly typical example of that view of the Atonement which we have called the Classic Idea. It will be useful, in conclusion, to sum up briefly its essential features.

First, then, it must be emphasised that the work of atonement is regarded as carried through by God Himself; and this, not merely in the sense that God authorises, sanctions, and initiates the plan of salvation, but that He Himself is the effective agent in the redemptive work, from beginning to end. It is the Word of God incarnate who overcomes the tyrants which hold man in bondage; God Himself enters into the world of sin and death, that He may reconcile the world to Himself. Therefore Incarnation and Atonement stand in no sort of antithesis; rather, they belong inseparably together. It is God's Love, the Divine *agape*, that removes the sentence that rested upon mankind, and creates a new relation between the human race and Himself, a relation which is altogether different from any sort of justification by legal righteousness. The whole dispensation is the work of grace. "Mankind, that had fallen into captivity, is now by God's mercy delivered out of the power of them that held them in bondage. God had mercy upon His creation, and bestowed upon them a new salvation through His Word, that is, Christ, so that men might learn by experience that they cannot attain to incorruption of themselves, but by God's grace only."[35]

Second, it is to be emphasised that this view of the Atonement has regularly a dualistic background—namely, the reality of forces of evil, which are hostile to the Divine will.

[35] *Adv. Hær.*, V., 21. 3.

Consequently, so far as the sphere of these forces extends, there is enmity between God and the world. The work of atonement is therefore depicted in dramatic terms, as a conflict with the powers of evil and a triumph over them. This involves a necessary double-sidedness, in that God is at once the Reconciler and the Reconciled. His enmity is taken away in the very act in which He reconciles the world unto Himself.

In the next chapter we shall pass from Irenæus to the later Fathers. We shall see how repeatedly and how powerfully his central ideas recur in their teaching. We shall be constantly meeting the same general teaching, under various forms of expression, like a series of variations on a theme. But variations have an interest of their own.

3

THE FATHERS IN EAST AND WEST

I. A GENERAL SURVEY

IT IS not possible, in the rapid summary to which we are obliged to confine ourselves, to treat all the Fathers as fully as we have treated Irenæus; nor is it necessary. In spite of all the diversities of the different Fathers, the general agreement between them on this subject is such that it is possible to treat them together in a single comprehensive statement. Indeed, attempts such as that of M. Rivière, in *Le dogme de la Rédemption*,[1] to distinguish clearly defined sub-varieties cannot fairly be maintained. He seeks to distinguish three different theories of the Atonement among the Fathers: first, a 'juridical' view, where the idea is of a ransom-price paid to the devil; second, a 'political' view, according to which the devil loses his dominion through misusing his rights over Christ, over whom he had no authority; and third, a more 'poetical' view—M. Rivière is here thinking of the common language about the deception of the devil, and the realistic images in which this idea is expressed. But in reality no such classification is possible. For one reason, it is inadequate to cover the ground, since there are other modes of treatment which M. Rivière does not mention; and for another, the ideas which he distinguishes frequently occur side by side in

1 See Rashdall, p. 365.

the same writer. In fact, there are not different theories of the Atonement in the Fathers, but only variant expressions of one and the same basic idea.

Nor, again, is it possible to agree with H. Mandel,[2] who in other respects has a much clearer grasp of the classic idea of the Atonement than most writers on the subject, in distinguishing two stages in the thought of the Greek Fathers: an earlier 'cosmological-ontological' and a later 'ethical-religious' stage. Mandel says that in the later stage sin, death, and the devil are no longer regarded in a purely cosmological-ontological way, that corruption now comes to be regarded as something more than merely physical, and that mortality is now treated as the consequence of sin. But all this is equally true of the earlier period, as we have seen in our study of Irenæus; and indeed, if such a distinction must be made, it would really be preferable to say that, at least in certain regions of the early church, a cosmological-ontological view gains ground in the later period at the expense of the other. In any case, Mandel's distinction of the two stages cannot be upheld.

If now we ask how widely spread was the classic idea of the Atonement in the early church, it may be definitely laid down that it dominates the whole of Greek patristic theology from Irenæus to John of Damascus, who is commonly regarded as marking the close of the patristic period, and has since been the standard authority in the Greek Orthodox Church. In all the Greek Fathers we find, in fact, amid some diversity of terms and images, one and the same dramatic view of the meaning of Christ's redemptive work. To mention only the most important names, Origen, Athanasius, Basil the Great, Gregory of Nyssa, Gregory of Nazianzus, Cyril of Alexandria, Cyril of Jerusalem, and Chrysostom represent different schools of thought and differ much from

[2] *Christliche Versöhnungslehre*, pp. 217 ff.

one another, as, for instance, in their attitudes towards Greek philosophy—but however we classify their differences from one another, we still find a deep-lying agreement in their interpretation of Christ's work. It is, indeed, significant that even those who are most strongly influenced by Greek philosophy, such as Origen and the two Cappadocian Gregories, take essentially the same view of the Atonement as the 'unphilosophical' Athanasius.

Attempts have been made with regard to Origen, as, for instance, by de Faye in his important work on Origen, to minimise the importance of this side of his teaching, and to treat it as belonging to a lower theological level, as if it were a mere appendage to the philosophically inclined system in which we find the real Origen. It may be remarked that the assumption that certain sides of a man's teaching must have been of less importance *to himself* is one that deserves to be severely criticised. In the case of Origen, even if the assumption were better justified than it is, the fact still remains that when he speaks directly of the meaning of Christ's work, he adopts the same classic idea of the Atonement which is common to the Greek Fathers. The fact that even philosophical influence was not able, either in his case or in others, to modify the classic idea of the Atonement, shows how deeply rooted it was in the teaching of the Greek Fathers.

The matter is, however, more complicated when we turn to the West. Here it is possible to discern **relatively early** the first traces of the typical Latin view of the Atonement, which was to find its full and clear formulation in the great work of Anselm; and we can fix precisely the point where it first emerges. We shall return to this subject in Chapter V.; for the present it will be enough to say that Tertullian, whose teaching about Penance centres altogether round the satisfaction made by man for sin and the idea of merit, begins to quarry the stones for the future edifice of the Latin theory, and that Cyprian first applies the ideas of Tertullian directly to the Atonement. After Cyprian, the Latin idea is to be found here and there in the Western Church, and increasingly as time goes on. Nevertheless, during the patristic period the Latin doctrine was never fully worked out, much less set consciously in opposition to the classic idea; for points belonging properly to the two different types of view often stand side by side without any apparent consciousness on the part of those who use them of their essential diversity. The classic type of view is dominant; the ideas of the Latin type have the character of tentative suggestions, which, however, gradually work their way forward in concealed opposition to the dominant classic teaching. But the investigation of the relations of the two types of view during this period requires far greater caution than is usually shown. Nothing is more common than to find points which really belong to the classic idea treated as if they were anticipations of the theory of Anselm.

Thus the classic idea of the Atonement is the dominant view of the Western as of the Eastern Fathers. We find it in Ambrose, pseudo-Ambrose, Augustine, Leo the Great, Cæsarius of Arles, Faustus of Rhegium, and Gregory the Great. Of these writers, Augustine and Gregory call for some further remarks.

The fact that Augustine accepts the classic idea of the Atonement is specially significant on account of his theological importance. There is no reason to seek to minimise the importance of this fact, as Harnack does, by branding these ideas of Augustine as "relics of common Catholicism," and remarking in another passage that when Augustine escapes from the bondage of common Catholicism he always speaks "neuplatonisch und schlicht religiös."[1] The sneer implied in the term 'common Catholicism' may well be

[1] *Dogmengeschichte*, 4th edn., III., 203.

ignored; but the collocation of 'neoplatonic' and 'purely religious' suggests at once that Harnack is guilty of a misinterpretation. It would follow that the 'purely religious' element stands in opposition to the Christian element in Augustine's theology.

Two further points should also be noted: first, that in Augustine the 'dramatic' view of Christ's work is closely connected with his very clear teaching on the Incarnation, and that it was at this point that Neoplatonism appeared to him to fail most completely. When, therefore, we take into account on the one hand the central importance of the Incarnation to Augustine, and on the other the intimate connection in his writing between the Incarnation and the dramatic view of the Atonement, it becomes clear that it is wholly arbitrary to brand this view of the Atonement as a less essential part of his thought, or a mere relic of 'common Catholicism.' And, second, it is in his doctrine of Love that Neoplatonic influence is chiefly evident; and here the disturbing influence of the Neoplatonic idea of Eros prevented him from holding quite consistently to the typically Christian idea of the Divine Love proceeding from heaven and shedding itself abroad among men. Naturally enough, the presence of the idea of Eros involved a weakening of the dramatic view of the Atonement, which depends altogether on the idea of the coming of the Divine Love down from heaven; but in so far as this was the case, it was a weakening of the essential Christian teaching, not merely of 'relics of common Catholicism.' But we cannot follow out this point further here. Our immediate concern is to see that whenever Augustine treats of Christ's redemptive work his thought belongs in all essentials to the classic type.

In Gregory the Great the classic idea of the Atonement finds vigorous expression. He pictures the drama of redemption in lurid colours. Many realistic and even grotesque images had been employed in the previous centuries to illustrate this theme, but Gregory outdoes all his predecessors. The fact that the classic idea holds this place in Gregory's writings is all the more remarkable because of his share in moulding the later mediæval idea of the sacrifice of the Mass; and there can be no doubt that this idea, as then commonly held, with a constant emphasis on an offering made by man to God, tended in the direction of the Latin doctrine of the Atonement. We do, in fact, find in Gregory a number of points which properly belong to the Latin view of the Atonement, side by side with the realistic imagery of the drama of redemption.[4]

Gregory's use of the classic idea was particularly important for the subsequent period; for his writings were assiduously read during the Middle Ages, and it is probable that Gregory had more influence than any other writer in preserving the classic idea in existence, and preventing its disappearance. When we add that Gregory was one of the patristic authors most studied by Luther, we may have part of the explanation of Luther's characteristic teaching on the Atonement. Certainly in Luther a number of his most realistic images reappear.

2. THE INCARNATION AND THE ATONEMENT

It is usually said that the main theological effort of the early church was exerted in the sphere of Christology; and this is true, in so far as its most monumental result is seen in the formulæ of the ecumenical councils. But it is not always clearly understood that the Christological definitions were worked out in close connection with a quite definite view of Christ's redemptive work, which, though it found no explicit place in the definitions, was present in the background

[4] *Cf.* p. 83, below.

throughout.[5] The Christology sets forth the paradoxical union of Godhead and manhood in Christ; the idea of redemption gives the reason why the subject was felt to be all-important.

The organic connection of the idea of the Incarnation with that of the Atonement is the leading characteristic of the doctrine of redemption in the early church. The central thought is the same that we have already seen in Irenæus; it is God Himself who enters into this world of sin and death for man's deliverance, to take up the conflict with the powers of evil and effect atonement between Himself and the world. Gregory of Nazianzus sums up the purpose of the Incarnation thus "that God, by overcoming the tyrant, might set us free and reconcile us with Himself through His Son."

Athanasius and Augustine discuss at length the answer to the question *Cur Deus homo?* The treatise of Athanasius *On the Incarnation of the Word* is wholly occupied with this subject. He argues that through the transgression sin has subjected the race of men to death's power, and on this account death has legal rights over men. But God's purpose cannot come to naught; for His love for the fallen race persists in spite of the judgment upon them. Therefore the Word becomes man, that He may restore the life which had been lost; for this was the one possible way, that Life, the Life of God, should enter into the world of men and prevail over death.

It is evident that such a view must lay emphasis not merely on the death of Christ, but also on His victory, His triumph, His passage through death to life. According to Anselm,

---

[5] *Cf.* Thornton, *The Incarnate Lord*, pp. 311–316. "What determined the issue in the fourth century was not this question of words (Logos or Son), but the demands of soteriology. Irenæus and Athanasius (in his earlier phase) had both linked the Logos terminology to a profoundly objective doctrine of redemption. . . . The Christology of Athanasius . . . was already settled by his conception of Christ as the Redeemer" (p. 311).

Christ became man primarily in order that He might die; but this isolation of the death of Christ is impossible for the patristic view. Death is, indeed, the way by which the victory is won, but the emphasis lies on the victory. Therefore the note of triumph sounds like a trumpet-call through the teaching of the early church.

But here we must stop to face a question which we had to ask in our study of Irenæus. Can it truly be said that Athanasius and his successors emphasise the thought of deliverance from death and from death's power, at the expense of that of deliverance from sin? Do they give us, as we are so often told, a 'physical' doctrine of salvation? It is specially relevant to ask this question while we are thinking of Athanasius, because he frequently dwells on the thought of deliverance from the power of death, but makes less mention of the devil than almost any of the Fathers; and there are a number of passages in his writings which, if taken in isolation, might easily suggest that he really does neglect the idea of sin. Thus in one place[6] he asks whether God could have adopted some other way than that of the Incarnation, and replies that for the gaining of salvation it might well have been sufficient that man should repent, if the only problem had been that of sin, and not of corruption and death as the consequence of sin; but since through sin men had lost the Divine image, and become subject to death, on this account the Word must come and deliver them from the power of corruption. From such passages it might appear that the need for Christ's coming and His redemptive work had arisen exclusively out of the consequences of sin, and not out of the sin itself; and so, that the work of Christ had only an indirect relation to sin.

But such an interpretation would not be just either to Athanasius or to the other Greek Fathers. Athanasius does,

6 *On the Incarnation of the Word*, ch. 7.

in fact, regard sin as not merely the cause of the corruption from which men need to be saved, but as being identical with it. That is to say, Christ's work has a direct relation to sin; He came in order that He might break the power of sin over human life. He came "that He might set all free from sin and the curse of sin, and that all might evermore live in truth, free from death, and be clothed in incorruption and immortality."[1] It may, indeed, be said that the forgiveness of sin is not proclaimed with the same power as by the Reformers; that the Greek theologian does not sound the depths like Luther. But this does not justify the allegation that the idea of sin takes only a subordinate place, and that his conception of salvation is purely 'physical' and 'natural,' the bestowal of immortality on human nature through the Divine nature of Christ. If the thought of the triumph of life and the overcoming of mortality takes the central place, it is intimately connected with the breaking of sin's power. The work of Christ is the overcoming of death *and* sin; strictly, it is a victory over death because it is a victory over sin. And, further, the note of triumph which rings through this Greek theology depends not only on the victory of Christ over death accomplished once for all, but also on the fact that His victory is the starting-point for His present work in the world of men, where He, through His Spirit, ever triumphantly continues to break down sin's power and 'deifies' men.

The Greek Fathers frequently discuss whether God could not have saved men by some other way than that of the drama of the Incarnation and Redemption, and, in particular, whether He could not have chosen to exert His power, and by His almighty *fiat* overthrow the tyrants and restore the fallen. Various answers are given. Athanasius replies that the Deliverance becomes effective in a wholly different way

[1] *Against the Arians*, II., 69.

when it is accomplished, as it were, from within, by God taking manhood, and not from without.[8] Again, it is frequently said that God's righteousness would not have been manifested if He had used mere force; sometimes there is the implication that the devil has certain rights over men, which God respects. Thus John of Damascus writes that God could have accomplished His will by force, and saved men from the dominion of the tyrant by His almighty power; but then "the tyrant would have had cause of complaint, if after he had gained dominion over men, he had been compelled by force to give them up. Therefore God, who sympathises with men and loves them, and desires to proclaim the vanquished as victors, becomes man. . . ." The Greek Fathers find the deepest reason for God's action in an inner Divine necessity, the necessity imposed by His love. The argument that the devil has rights over men is not intended as a rational theory of the necessity for the drama of the Incarnation and Redemption; the writer moves in a wholly different plane from Anselm, whose whole preoccupation is with rational demonstration.

The same teaching about the Divine Love is dominant in Augustine. He shows that the race of men is delivered into the power of the devil on account of its sin; guilt rests on the whole race. Yet God does not cease to love mankind, and the Incarnation is the proof of the greatness of His love. His love could not be more clearly revealed than by the coming of His Son into fellowship with us, to take upon Himself our sufferings and the evil which rests upon us. Thereby we are saved, justified by His blood, reconciled to God through the death of His Son, delivered from the wrath.

This is Augustine's answer to the question *Cur Deus homo?* His treatment is more powerful than that of Athana-

[8] *Against the Arians*, II., 68.

sius, and his outlook wider, but the main idea is the same. The Incarnation has its basis in God's Love. The work of the Incarnate is the work of the Divine Love. This it is that overcomes the tyrants, and effects atonement between God and the world. It is one Divine work, the continuity of which is not interrupted by the idea of an offering made to God from man's side, from below.

This thought of God's coming to man to save is expressed with remarkable clearness by Gregory of Nyssa: "It is of the nature of fire to tend upwards, and no one finds anything strange when it thus takes its natural direction. But any who should see a tongue of flame shooting downwards would regard it as most surprising if the fire remained fire, and yet in its movement pointed in a direction which was contrary to its nature. Similarly, the invincibility of the Divine power is not so proved by the vastness of the heaven, the radiance of the stars, the orderliness of the universe, and the providential government of all things, as it is proved by its condescension to the weakness of our nature. The lofty stoops to the lowly without losing its loftiness, the Divine nature unites itself with the human nature, and becomes human, without ceasing to be Divine. . . . It is the nature of light to drive away darkness, and of life to overcome death. When now we had from the beginning strayed from the right way, and turned away from life to death, what impossibility is there in the mystery that teaches us that Purity has stooped down to them that were defiled with sin, Life to them that were dead, the Guide to them that had gone astray, that the defiled might be made clean, the dead raised, and the wanderers led back to the right way?"[9] This passage is of special interest because its emphasis on the Divine act of redemption occurs in a context where the deception of the devil is depicted in realistic language; it therefore reveals the religious

[9] *Great Catechism*, ch. 24, 1 and 2.

background of such grotesque imagery. To this we must now turn.

3. CHRIST AND THE DEVIL

No other aspect of the teaching of the Fathers on the subject of Redemption has provoked such criticism as their treatment of the dealings of Christ with the devil; primarily on this ground, their teaching has been commonly regarded as unworthy of serious consideration. The judgment that Anselm marks a great advance on the early church doctrine rests chiefly on this, that he is regarded as having overcome the idea of a transaction with the devil, as well as the grotesque idea of a deception of the devil. Nothing is more common than to find the patristic teaching dismissed with an impatient shrug of the shoulders, as mere puerilities, or sharply rated as ethically intolerable. So Rashdall writes: "The objectionable feature in the whole system is not the mere use of the term 'ransom,' or of the expression 'paid' or 'offered' or 'given' to the Devil, but the treatment of the Devil's supposed dominion over man as an assertion of just rights and a lawful jurisdiction, and the childish and immoral way in which these rights were satisfied or bought out by Christ's death."[10]

It must be admitted that it is not surprising that many features in the patristic teaching should awaken disgust, such as its mythological dress, its naïve simplicity, its grotesque realism. But it may well be questioned whether it is justifiable on this account to cast this teaching summarily aside. It should be evident that the historical study of dogma is wasting its time in pure superficiality if it does not endeavour to penetrate to that which lies below the outward dress, and look for the religious values which lie concealed underneath.

Rashdall's objections are to be found stated, in part, in the

10 *The Idea of Atonement in Christian Theology*, p. 364.

patristic writings themselves. The Fathers are by no means
all of one mind on the subject of Christ's dealings with Satan,
and on some points they differ sharply from one another.
All agree that the devil was rightly and reasonably overcome; the teaching of Irenæus is typical, that man was
created by God to belong to Him, that the devil's dominion
over man is a perversion of the right order, that the Creator
is one with the Redeemer.[11] The differences appear on the
subject of the devil's rights over man and the manner of
Christ's dealings with the devil. The most common view is
that since the Fall the devil possesses an incontestable right
over fallen man, and that therefore a regular and orderly
settlement is necessary; but sometimes this view is traversed
by another, which regards the devil as a usurper, and therefore as possessing no sort of right over men. Both forms of
teaching can, however, speak of the devil as having been
deceived by God or by Christ; this idea enjoyed great popularity, and seems to have met with little serious criticism.

Gregory of Nyssa, who discusses with especial fulness
this subject of Christ's dealings with the devil, plainly asserts
that the devil acquired rights over mankind through the
Fall. Here he is really following Athanasius, who had spoken
of death as having lawful dominion over men; the difference
is little more than that 'the devil' is substituted for 'death.'
The religious motive lying behind the mythological language is plainly *the desire to assert the guilt of mankind, and
the judgment of God on human sin.*

But Gregory is at the same time anxious to show the right-
fulness of the deliverance of man from the devil's power.
The deliverance is the work of God's Love, but also of His
Wisdom and His Righteousness; God does not effect His
purpose by sheer force. Gregory takes an analogy from
slavery and emancipation: if a slave is set free by an act of

11 See p. 27 f., above.

violence, then he is not rightfully set free. "The case was similar, when we of our own freewill had sold ourselves, and God in His goodness would restore us again to freedom. There was a kind of necessity for Him not to proceed by way of force, but to accomplish our deliverance in a lawful way. It consists in this, that the owner is offered all that he asks as the redemption-price of His property."[12]

This is the very favourite image of the Ransom. The price of the life of Christ, paid as ransom for men, is commonly regarded as paid to the devil, or to death; and this is the natural suggestion of the image. Origen discusses to whom the ransom-price is paid, and directly denies that it can possibly be paid to God.[13] "But to whom did He give His soul as a ransom for many? Surely not to God. Could it, then, be to the Evil One? For he had us in his power, until the ransom for us should be given to him, even the life (or soul) of Jesus, since he (the Evil One) had been deceived, and led to suppose that he was capable of mastering that soul, and he did not see that to hold Him involved a trial of strength (βάσανον) greater than he was equal to. Therefore also death, though he thought he had prevailed against Him, no longer lords it over Him, He (Christ) having become free among the dead and stronger than the power of death, and so much stronger than death that all who will amongst those who are mastered by death may also follow Him (i.e., out of Hades, out of death's domain), death no longer prevailing against them. For every one who is with Jesus is unassailable by death."

But this teaching of a ransom-price paid to the devil was directly challenged by Gregory of Nazianzus, who denied that the devil could have any real rights over men, and

---

[12] *Great Catechism*, ch. 22.
[13] *In Matthæum*, xvi. 8. Translation from Rashdall, p. 259, where the Greek is printed in full.

therefore rejected any notion of a transaction with him. How could a ransom be paid to the devil? A price is paid for the emancipation of a slave; and though undeniably men were under the power of the devil, and thus it might seem plausible that a ransom should be paid to him, nothing of the sort can really have happened. It is not fitting that the devil, who is a robber, should receive a price in return for what he had taken by violence, and a price of such value as the Son of God Himself. The devil had no rights; on the contrary, it was altogether right that he should be conquered and forced to surrender his prey. In the end Gregory of Nazianzus rejects the idea of ransom altogether; he will not allow that a ransom was paid to the devil, nor yet to God,[14] for, as he says, we were not in bondage under God. He prefers to use the idea of sacrifice.

Thus the idea of a transaction with the devil met with strong criticism; nevertheless, it was firmly established in the early church, and it constantly recurs in the Fathers. Very commonly we read that the devil exceeded his rights in his treatment of Christ, and therefore was deprived of his rights and lost his kingdom. Thus Chrysostom, commenting on John xii. 31,[15] writes: "It is as if Christ said, 'Now shall a trial be held, and a judgment be pronounced. How and in what manner? He (the devil) smote the first man, because he found him guilty of sin; for it was through sin that death entered in. But he did not find any sin in Me; wherefore then did he fall on Me and give Me up to the power of death? . . . How is the world now judged in Me?' It is as if it were said to the devil at a seat of judgment: 'Thou didst smite them all, because thou didst find them guilty of sin; wherefore then didst thou smite Christ? Is it not evident that

---

[14] That the ransom was paid to God is occasionally asserted, as by John of Damascus. *Cf.* p. 56, below.

[15] "Now is the judgment of this world: now shall the prince of this world be cast out."

thou didst this wrongfully? Therefore the whole world shall become righteous through Him.' "

Chrysostom uses other images also. The devil is like a tyrant who tortures those who fall into his hands; but now he meets a king or a king's son, whom he unjustly beats to death. His death then leads to the deliverance of the others. Or, the devil is compared to a creditor, who casts into prison those who are in debt to him; but now he imprisons one who owes him nothing. He has exceeded his rights, and he is deprived of his dominion. Similar illustrations occur frequently; thus Augustine says that the devil found Christ innocent, but none the less smote Him; he shed innocent blood, and took what he had no right to take. Therefore it is fitting that he should be dethroned and forced to give up those who were under his power. We may note in passing that the same idea comes often in Luther. In words which are strongly reminiscent of Chrysostom (whom he also explicitly quotes), Luther teaches that 'the Law,' which had claimed dominion over Christ, over whom it had no right, is brought to judgment and deprived of the position of 'tyrant' which formerly it held.

But it is the idea of the deception of the devil that provides occasion for the use of the most realistic imagery. The theme on which the variations are made is that Christ appears as it were *incognito*, His Godhead being hidden under His human nature; hence the devil thinks that He will be an easy prey. Traces of this idea occur in Irenæus[16] and in Origen,[17] who quotes 1 Cor. ii. 7–8: "We speak God's wisdom in a mystery . . . which none of the rules of this world knoweth: for had they known it, they would not have cru-

---

[16] See p. 25, above.

[17] Origen has also the idea that Christ, the Son of the rightful King, disguises Himself as an ordinary man, in order that He may the more easily persuade the devil's prisoners to follow Him out of the prison-house.

cified the Lord of glory." But Gregory of Nyssa develops
this idea in greater detail than any before him. When the
Godhead clothes itself in human form, the devil thinks that
he sees a uniquely desirable prey; the Godhead in Christ is
so hidden that he does not notice the danger which threatens
him, and which under other circumstances he would immediately have avoided. Therefore he accepts the offered
prey; as a fish swallows the bait on the fish-hook, so the
devil swallows his prey, and is thereby taken captive by the
Godhead, hidden under the human nature. "Since the hostile
power was not going to enter into relations with a God
present unveiled, or endure His appearance in heavenly
glory, therefore God, in order to render Himself accessible
to him who demanded of Him a ransom for us, concealed
Himself under the veil of our nature, in order that, as happens with greedy fishes, together with the bait of the flesh
the hook of the Godhead might also be swallowed, and so,
through Life passing over into death, and the Light arising
in the darkness, that which is opposed to Life and Light
might be brought to nought. For darkness cannot endure
when the Light shines, nor can death remain in being where
Life is active."[18]

Gregory admits that there are objections to thus describing God's action; as we have seen, he had strongly maintained that idea of the devil's rights over mankind, and his
consequent demand for justice. But he takes great pains to
show that God's action does not in fact conflict with His
wisdom and His righteousness, and that no injustice is done
to the devil: "Drugs can be mixed with food either by an
enemy or by a physician desiring to heal his patient. The
one does it to cause death, the other as an antidote; and this
method of healing is not inconsistent with a beneficent purpose. For if both drug the food, we must have regard to the

[18] *Great Catechism*, ch. 24.

motive when we praise the one and blame the other. Therefore it is nothing but just when he who led us astray is paid
back in his own coin; for just as he at the beginning beguiled men with the bait of fleshly lust, he is now beguiled
through God clothing Himself in the veil of humanity. But
the purpose which God sought to attain brings it about that
His action must be treated as good and just."[19]

This idea of the deception of the devil occurs frequently,
both in the East and in the West. Augustine uses the simile
of a mouse-trap; as the mice are enticed into the trap by the
bait, so Christ is the bait by which the devil is caught. Gregory the Great frequently enlarges on this theme, and his
imagery leaves nothing to be desired in the way of grotesque
realism. But we cannot follow this point out in further detail; for it is time to ask ourselves what are the religious
meanings which lie concealed under modes of presentation
which to us are so highly objectionable.

First, then, this whole group of ideas, including the semi-
legal transaction with the devil, the payment of the ransom-
price, and the deception, is presented, often explicitly, in
order to deny that God proceeds by way of brute force to
accomplish His purpose by compulsion. However crude the
form, the endeavour is to show that God does not stand, as
it were, outside the drama that is being played out, but Himself takes part in it, and attains His purpose by internal, not
by external, means; He overcomes evil, not by an almighty
fiat, but by putting in something of His own, through a
Divine self-oblation.

Second, the use of legal imagery to describe the transaction with the devil does not in any way mean that the relation between God, the world, and the devil is regarded
throughout from a legalistic standpoint. Rashdall speaks of
the 'quasi-legal' view of the Atonement. We may ignore the

---

[19] *Great Catechism,* ch. 26.

depreciatory tone of his language, and attend to its substance. The fact that these descriptions in the Fathers of an orderly, legal process alternate so strangely with those of the devil's deception is enough to show that there is no intention of comprehending the Divine action within a legal scheme. The case is quite different in the Fathers from what it became in the days of the Latin theory of the Atonement. The background of the Latin theory may truly be called legal; but in the Fathers the essential idea which the legal language is intended to express is that God's dealings even with the powers of evil have the character of 'fair play.' Thus this point connects itself closely with the last. Evil is overcome not by an external use of force, but by internal methods of self-offering.

Third, with regard to the devil's rights, it is important to observe the characteristic alternation of thought: on the one hand, the devil is an enemy, a beguiler, a usurper; on the other, he has won certain rights over man. The former idea is thoroughly dualistic; it gives us the conflict between God and the representative and embodiment of evil. The second shows the limitations of Dualism; for the devil is not a power equal and opposite to God, and in so far as he has power over men, he derives this power ultimately from God, for he stands, as it were, to execute God's own judgment on sinful and guilty man. The idea is at times expressed in very crude forms; but it is wholly unjustifiable for Rashdall and others to call the language of the Fathers about the devil's rights 'immoral.' The underlying idea is, in fact, the very opposite of immoral; for it asserts, fundamentally, the responsibility of man for his sin, and that the judgment which rests on mankind is a righteous judgment. If the Fathers are to be blamed, they ought not to be blamed on this ground, but rather because they never fully dared to trust themselves to maintain and assert clearly *both* sides of the case;

to assert at one and the same time that the devil is God's enemy, and that he is also the executant of God's judgment. We shall return to this point later.[20] But if this is right, Gregory of Nazianzus is scarcely to be complimented on his rejection of the idea of the payment of the ransom-price.

Fourth, with regard to the deception of the devil. It scarcely needs to be said that the application of any such thought to God is at least dangerous, and that the realistic expressions of it, if taken literally, are absurd. But we may remind ourselves that while Luther readily adopts these analogies, even in their most grotesque forms, he finds in them the starting-point for some of his deepest teachings about 'the hidden God.'[21] It is true that we do not find just this profundity of interpretation in the Fathers. Yet behind all the seemingly fantastic speculations lies the thought that the power of evil ultimately overreaches itself when it comes in conflict with the power of good, with God Himself. It loses the battle at the moment when it seems to be victorious.

4. THE DOUBLE ASPECT OF THE DRAMA OF THE ATONEMENT

A certain double-sidedness is an essential feature of the classic idea of the Atonement. On the one hand, the drama of Redemption has a dualistic background; God in Christ combats and prevails over the 'tyrants' which hold mankind in bondage. On the other hand, God thereby becomes reconciled with the world, the enmity is taken away, and a new relation between God and mankind is established. We saw how in Irenæus the victory of Christ brings to pass reconciliation between God and the world; but the double aspect comes out with increasing clearness in the later Fathers. It is now explicitly taught that the devil and death,

[20] See p. 56 f., below.   [21] See p. 110 below.

over which Christ wins His triumph, are also, from another point of view, the executants of God's judgment on sinful man. This brings out plainly the double aspect of the drama of redemption. God is at once the author and the object of the reconciliation; He is reconciled in the act of reconciling the world to Himself. The double-sidedness appears in most of the analogies used to illustrate the meaning of Christ's death.

The image of the ransom-price naturally relates itself to the powers of evil, for it is to these that the ransom is paid. Yet we find at times a reluctance to affirm this, and it can even at times be said that the ransom is paid to God. But such statements do not mean that a doctrine of the Latin type has displaced the classic idea of the Atonement; for this double-sidedness is essential to the classic idea. Deliverance from the powers of evil, death, and the devil is at the same time deliverance from God's judgment on sin.

The same is true of the image of Debt, which is parallel to the image of Ransom, but is much less frequently employed. Athanasius speaks of the Word of God as by the offering up of His body "paying the debt for all by His death," and that thereby death was "satisfied"; he also connects this thought with the idea of sacrifice, and says that "The Word gave the body which He took, as an oblation, as an undefiled sacrifice in death, and so removed death from all His brethren by His vicarious sacrifice."[22] The debt is regarded as paid primarily to death; but he can also say that a "debt of honour" is paid to God. The alternation of phrase means that it was the judgment of God's righteousness that subjected men to death. Athanasius is in no way forsaking the classic point of view; the payment of the debt is God's own act, carried out by the Logos, while at the same time it is God who receives the payment. Least

22 *On the Incarnation of the Word,* ch. 9.

of all is it true to say that we have here anything like a rational theory of the Latin type, according to which satisfaction would be paid to God's justice from man's side, from below. It is significant that in this very context Athanasius quotes Heb. ii. 14: "Since then the children are sharers in flesh and blood, He also Himself in like manner partook of the same, that through death He might bring to nought him that had the power of death, that is, the devil."

Again, even when the suffering which Christ endured is treated as the endurance of the punishment which men deserved, this is another instance of the same double aspect. When Christ suffers the punishment involved in God's judgment on sin, this is the accomplishment of God's own work of redemption, whereby the tyrants are overcome and the reconciliation takes place.

The same is seen in the use of the imagery of sacrifice. Harnack's contention that according to the Greek doctrine all is effected by the Incarnation alone, and that the idea of sacrifice is essentially alien to this doctrine,[28] does not correspond to the facts. The contrast between the Greek idea and the Latin, which Harnack is trying to find, would be better expressed somewhat as follows: That the typically Latin view of the Atonement always regards the sacrifice as offered by man to God, and works this out in a logical theory; but the classic idea of the Atonement, whether in the East or in the West, is always marked by a double-sidedness. The Sacrifice is the means whereby the tyrants are overcome; yet there is a close connection between the tyrants and God's own judgment on sin. The idea that God receives the sacrifice is not based on a theoretical calculation of what God must demand from man's side for the satisfaction of His justice before atonement can be effected. Rather the idea is that sacrifice stands in the Divine Economy

28 *History of Dogma*, III., 305.

as the means whereby the Divine will-to-reconciliation real-
ises itself, and which also shows how much it costs God to
effect the Atonement. One saying of Gregory of Nazianzus
is specially illuminating: "Is it not clear that the Father received the sacrifice, not because He Himself demanded it
or needed it, but only on account of the Divine economy
. . . that He Himself might deliver us, in overcoming the
tyrants by His power, and by the mediation of His Son
bringing us back to himself?"[24] Thus the sacrifice stands not
in an external but in an internal relation to God's will. Mandel, to whom I am indebted for the above quotation, thus
expresses the point: "It is God's ordinance and economy in
the world that the sinner belongs to perdition and to the
devil, and it is with this will of God that the sacrifice is in
the last resort concerned."[25]

In the West, Augustine takes essentially the same line.[26]
He speaks with more emphasis than the generality of the
Greek theologians of the judgment of God impending upon
mankind, but he does not on this account incline to a Latin
doctrine of the Atonement; on the contrary, he seems to
intend a pointed rejection of any such idea. He denies that
God the Father can be in any way 'placated' by the Son's
death; for in that case there would be a difference of some
kind, even a conflict, between the Father and the Son: but
that is unthinkable, for between the Father and the Son
there is always the most perfect harmony. Characteristically
enough, he bases his argument on the doctrines of the Incarnation and the Trinity.

The double-sidedness which we have observed in the
classic idea of the Atonement brings out one more contrast
between it and the Latin doctrine; for it makes it next to
impossible to construct a rationally consistent theory of the

[24] *Orat.*, 45.   [25] *Christliche Versöhnungslehre,* p. 219.
[26] See especially the *De Trinitate*, Bk. IV.

Atonement. The Latin doctrine, on the other hand, is in its very structure a rational theory; and from the point of view of this doctrine the classic idea must always seem to be lacking in clearness. It may be doubted, however, whether this demand for rational clearness represents the highest theological wisdom.

But in truth the classic idea of the Atonement, as it is set forth in the Fathers, is both clear and monumental. It sets forth God's coming to man, to accomplish His redemptive work; Incarnation and Redemption belong indissolubly together; God in Christ overcomes the hostile powers which hold man in bondage. At the same time these hostile powers are also the executants of God's will. The patristic theology is dualistic, but it is not an absolute Dualism. The deliverance of man from the power of death and the devil is at the same time his deliverance from God's judgment. God is reconciled by His own act in reconciling the world to Himself.

Thus the power of evil is broken; that is to say, not that sin and death no longer exist, but that, the devil having been once for all conquered by Christ, His triumph is in principle universal, and His redemptive work can go forward everywhere, through the Spirit who unites men with God and 'deifies' them; and in regard to death, Athanasius can say that the disciples of Christ no longer fear death, since death has no more dominion over them, but "by the sign of the cross and by faith in Christ they trample death to the ground as itself dead."[27] It can also be said that death is changed from an enemy to a friend.

Two points may be emphasised in conclusion. First, that the double-sidedness of the classic idea of the Atonement means that God is not only the Reconciler but also the Reconciled. It is not only that the world now stands in a new relation to God, but also that God stands in a new rela-

[27] *On the Incarnation of the Word*, ch. 27.

tion to the world. Thus the classic idea expresses a positive element which was later to be stressed in the Anselmian doctrine.

Secondly, in regarding the Atonement as God's own saving work, the Fathers do not lose sight of the fact that it is carried out in and through man. The Incarnation is the manifestation of God's goodness and the fulfilment of His saving work *in carne*, in the flesh, under the conditions of human nature. They repudiate the Apollinarian heresy, according to which the Logos takes the place of the human mind and soul in Christ, and the Monophysite heresy, according to which the human in Christ is merged into the Divine. Both these heresies deny the Pauline word, "Since by man came death, by man came also the resurrection of the dead." Thus in holding steadily fast to the true manhood of Christ, the orthodox theologians express the positive truth which afterwards the 'humanistic' doctrine endeavoured, not altogether successfully, to express, when it spoke of Christ as 'Representative Man.'

4

THE NEW TESTAMENT

I. INTERPRETATIONS OF THE NEW TESTAMENT TEACHING

IT IS evident that we have been guilty of an unjustifiable assumption in adopting the title of 'the classic idea of the Atonement,' if that idea is not, after all, the dominant idea in the canonical scriptures which are the classics of the Christian faith. To this extent it may be said that we have already assumed this conclusion. In any case it is difficult not to do this; it is undeniable that all the main interpretations of the Atonement have sought to base themselves on the New Testament. To the representatives of the Latin doctrine—Anselm and still more the theologians of the seventeenth century—it was entirely self-evident that their doctrine was the scriptural doctrine.

But, regarding the matter purely objectively, and reckoning up the a priori probabilities of the case, it is clear that *if* the classic idea of the Atonement dominated the whole patristic period, whereas the Latin doctrine only began to emerge in the West during that period, and did not attain its complete expression till the Middle Ages, *then* it is altogether likely that the classic idea will be found to be firmly rooted in Apostolic Christianity. It would be in the last degree improbable that an idea of the Atonement which was unrepresented in the Apostolic Age should suddenly emerge in the early church and there win universal acceptance. We are, then, justified in approaching our consideration of the New Testament evidence with this a priori probability in mind.

If it is true in general that the Atonement has for centuries past been studied from the point of view of either acceptance or rejection of the orthodox satisfaction-theory, this is particularly true of New Testament exegesis. As we have just said, the theologians of Protestant Orthodoxy took it completely for granted that the theory of the satisfaction of God's justice was to be found everywhere in the New Testament, or, rather, that it was presupposed both in the New Testament and in the Old; in fact, it was primarily from the Old Testament that the 'scriptural proofs' of the Atonement were primarily drawn, and this is a highly significant point. In the New Testament special weight was laid upon the Pauline teaching—above all, on cardinal passages such as Rom. iii. 24: "Being justified freely by His grace through the redemption that is in Christ Jesus: whom God set forth to be a propitiation, through faith, by His blood, to show His righteousness, because of the passing over of the sins done aforetime, in the forbearance of God." It was taken as certain that the satisfaction-theory underlay this passage, and every other allusion to redemption or to sacrifice, and every reference to the blood of Christ, or that Christ died for our sins, or suffered for our sake or in our stead.

The champions of the 'subjective' or exemplarist view joined issue at this point. Discussion raged round the Pauline doctrine; it was in reference to the doctrine of redemption that the nineteenth-century discussions of the relation between Jesus and Paul were most acute. Sometimes the liberal theologians accepted the orthodox interpretation of the

Pauline teaching; in this case Paul was taken to be the real author of the Anselmian doctrine of the Atonement, and his theology as marking the beginning of a decline from the original and authentic Christianity of the Gospel. Sometimes the great Apostle was treated with more respect; and in this case a strong tendency appeared towards a modernising interpretation of his teaching. It was claimed that his teaching could not be wholly summed up in the theory of satisfaction, and efforts were made to find points of contact with the 'subjective' view. Or, again, attempts were made to deal with Paul by distinguishing between his theology and his religion, with a decided preference for the latter; his theology was treated as secondary and less essential, all the more because it was developed for controversial purposes, and was largely dependent on the forms in which the problem was stated by his judaising opponents. A typical example may be found in A. Deissmann's book, *The Religion of Jesus and the Faith of Paul.* Here it is said that the great fault of Pauline exegesis has been that "Paul has been carried across from his original sphere, that of living religion, to the sphere of theology, which, though it is not wholly alien to him, is nevertheless clearly secondary." Deissmann asks whether the emphasis ought to be laid on Paul's personal relation to Christ or on his Christology, thus assuming a sharp contrast between the two.

We have every right to question this distinction. It is indeed true that Paul is not a scholastic theologian, and that the old assumption, that there is to be found in him a fully articulated theological system, is unsound. But the distinction between the religion of Paul and his theology seems to imply that for him the content of his faith was relatively secondary and unessential; and this is manifestly impossible. In fact, this distinction between his religion and his theology, which has seemed to such writers to be both clear and necessary, is in reality very far indeed from being clear; it is based on the very unclear idea of nineteenth-century liberalism on the relation between faith and the content of faith. The next stage is that Paul begins to be treated as a 'mystic,' and this ambiguous word produces its usual effect of fogging and obscuring the problem at issue.

But recent years have seen something of a revolution in New Testament exegesis. The school of Comparative Religion, if this term be taken in its widest sense, deserves a large share of the credit for the change. These scholars have not, indeed, been free from a certain arrogance, yet they may justly claim to have provided a real escape from doctrinaire methods of interpretation, both from those of orthodoxy on the one side and those of liberalism on the other. The new methods have had their faults, as is generally recognised; there has been too great readiness to be content with analogies drawn from other religions, and to fail to penetrate to the deeper meanings of the Christian writings. But such failings must not be allowed to obscure the great gains which the new methods have brought. In place of the modernising exegesis of liberalism, the 'primitive' features of Apostolic Christianity have been emphasised with great vigour, the features which stand in such sharp contrast with the outlook of the modern man. The new radical exegesis has felt itself to be most definitely challenging nineteenth-century liberal Protestantism; but this has not involved a return to the conservative outlook. In actual fact, our eyes have been opened to perceive certain important features of primitive Christianity, which were equally hidden from the conservatism and from the liberalism of the nineteenth century; such, for instance, as the decisive importance of the eschatological outlook in the New Testament. But at the same time new light is being thrown on the ideas of salvation and atonement in the Apostolic Age.

So far as I am able to judge, the first book to express the new outlook with full clearness was W. Wrede's small but much-discussed book *Paulus*, which first appeared in 1904. It contains much that is highly disputable; nevertheless, it surveys the problem with a masterly clearness which later writers on the subject have in many cases failed to achieve. Two points are of special importance for our present purpose. First, Wrede saw the unsatisfactoriness of the accepted opposition between Paul's religion and his theology: "Theology," he says, "is in no way secondary to Paul; it cannot be regarded as an interpretation, or an objectivising, of his experiences." "The religion of the Apostle is thoroughly theological; his theology is his religion."[1] Wrede's meaning is that Paul knows that he has a perfectly definite message to proclaim, and that the content of the message is not secondary, but, on the contrary, all-important.

Second, Wrede makes a determined attempt to envisage Paul's teaching as a whole. It is not intelligible as a patchwork; it all groups itself round one central point, and that point is Redemption. Paul regards men as held in bondage under objective powers of evil; namely, first of all, the 'flesh,' sin, the Law, death. These are no mere abstracts or metaphorical expressions, but *Wesenheiten*, realities, active forces. Secondly, Paul speaks of another order of powers of evil, demons, principalities, powers, which bear rule in this world, God having permitted them for the time being to have dominion. Satan stands at the head of the demonic powers. The purpose of Christ's coming is to deliver men from all these powers of evil. He descends from heaven, and becomes subject to the powers of this world, that finally He may overcome them by His death and resurrection. The demonic powers "crucify the Lord of glory"—so Wrede interprets I Cor. ii. 6—but through that very act they are defeated, and

[1] P. 48.

in the Resurrection Christ passes on into the new life. The
work of Christ avails for all; as "one died for all, therefore
all died," so through His triumph all are set free from the
power of evil. Wrede emphasises particularly that the Resurrection is as important as the death; if Paul spends more time
in explaining the meaning of the death, it is because the Resurrection explains itself. "Christ the Son of God relinquishes
His Sonship and becomes a poor man, like unto us, that we
men might become God's sons; Christ descends into the
sphere of sin, and overcomes it by His death, that thereby
we, who were languishing in bondage to sin, might be set
free—such phrases express the pith of his meaning."[2] It can
hardly be disputed that such exegesis represents something
altogether essential to Paul's message.

2. THE DRAMA OF REDEMPTION IN THE PAULINE
EPISTLES

Our consideration of the different interpretations of the
idea of atonement in the New Testament has led us to Paul;
and we shall be compelled to devote what might seem to be
a disproportionate amount of space to his teaching, because
his teaching has been the centre of controversy, and it has
been commonly believed that he is the real founder of the
Latin doctrine of the Atonement. But if Wrede is right, the
Pauline teaching belongs neither to the 'orthodox' or Latin
type, nor to the 'subjective' or liberal type; it really hangs
closely together with the view that we have studied in the
Fathers, and belongs to the classic type. There is the same
dualistic outlook, the same idea of conflict and triumph; of
powers of evil under which mankind is in bondage; of the
victory over them won by a Christ come down from heaven
—that is, by God Himself come to save. It is not a logically
articulated *theory* of redemption, but rather an idea, a *motif*,

2 P. 65.

a theme, which is essentially one and the same in Paul and in the early church, but finds ever-varying forms of expression.

What, then, are the chief differences between the expression of the classic idea of atonement in Paul and in the Fathers?

First, we may note that while he, like them, groups together sin and death, and connects them inseparably together, he makes considerably less mention of the devil than most of the Fathers; instead, in some important passages he speaks of a great complex of demonic forces, "principalities and powers," which Christ has overcome in the great conflict. Then, again, among the powers which hold man in bondage he ranges the Law; and this is the most striking point of contrast between his view and that of the Fathers. The triumph of Christ is the dethroning of Law and the deliverance of man from bondage to it.

With regard to the collocation of sin and death, we need only speak briefly. Sin takes the central place among the powers which hold man in bondage; all the others stand in direct relation to it. Above all, death, which is sometimes almost personified, as "the last enemy that shall be destroyed" (1 Cor. xv. 26), is most closely connected with sin. Where sin reigns, there death reigns also. To be set free from sin through Christ is to be delivered also from death's dominion; the salvation won by Christ has come "unto all men to justification of life" (Rom. v. 18); "even so reckon ye also yourselves to be dead unto sin, but alive unto God in Christ Jesus" (Rom. vi. 11).

The very striking fact that Paul counts the Law among the powers which hold mankind in bondage brings us to the same double-sidedness which we found in the classic idea of atonement in the Fathers, but in a still more acute form. In the patristic teaching, death and the devil are at once powers hostile to God and executants of God's judgment on sin. In the Pauline teaching, the Law of God itself is in one aspect a hostile power. On the one side, it is "holy and righteous and good"; on the other, "the sting of death is sin, and the power of sin is the Law" (1 Cor. xv. 56), and "as many as are of the works of the Law are under a curse" (Gal. iii. 10).

That the Law is counted as a hostile power does not depend only or chiefly on the fact that the Law inexorably condemns sin. The real reason lies deeper. The way of legal righteousness which the Law recommends, or, rather, demands, can never lead to salvation and life. It leads, like the way of human merit, not to God, but away from God, and deeper and deeper into sin; "to him that worketh, the reward is not reckoned as of grace, but as of debt" (Rom. iv. 4), and "when the commandment came, sin revived, and I died" (Rom. vii. 9). Thus the Law is an enemy, from whose tyranny Christ has come to save us: "Wherefore, my brethren, ye also were made dead to the Law through the body of Christ, that ye should be joined to another, even to Him who was raised from the dead" (Rom. vii. 4); "Christ redeemed us from the curse of the Law" (Gal. iii. 13); He has "blotted out the bond written in ordinances that was against us, and He hath taken it out of the way, nailing it to the cross" (Col. ii. 14). So Christ is "the end of the Law unto righteousness" (Rom. x. 4); the Law, as an enemy, is overcome.

Such texts express in the most pointed way Paul's opposition to Judaism and to all legalistic religion. The fact that Christ brings the Law to an end means that the righteousness of Law can no longer say the last decisive word in regard to the relation between God and the world. The Divine Love cannot be imprisoned in the categories of merit and of justice; it breaks them in pieces.

It is significant that this feature of the Pauline teaching is distinctly weakened in the Fathers, and even in the later New Testament writings; it does not, in fact, return in full strength till Martin Luther. It is true that the Fathers think of the Atonement as a continuous Divine work, and that the Atonement cannot possibly be comprehended in a legal scheme of merit and of justice; for the classic idea of the Atonement is always anti-moralistic, and it did, in fact, form the surest safeguard of the early church against moralism. Nevertheless, the early church certainly lost something of the elemental vigour of the Pauline conception; the bestowal of grace ceased to appear altogether paradoxical. Perhaps an important part of the explanation is to be found in the controversy against Marcion. Marcion exaggerated the Pauline teaching about the Law to the point of caricature; anti-moralism with him became sheer antinomianism. He entirely failed to maintain the double aspect of the conception of the Law as on the one hand holy and righteous and good, and on the other an instrument of bondage; he condemned the Law *in toto*, and the necessary opposition of the church theologians drove them into reaction on the other side, and robbed them of some of the force of the Pauline conception. But it must be admitted that this controversy only reinforced a tendency which was already operative independently.

The array of hostile forces includes also the complex of demonic 'Principalities,' 'Powers,' 'Thrones,' 'Dominions,' which rule in "this present evil age" (Gal. i. 4, R.V. mg.), but over which Christ has prevailed. There is comparatively little direct mention of the devil, but he is without doubt regarded as standing behind the demonic hosts as their chief. Particularly in Colossians the theme of Christ's victory over the demonic powers is of primary importance; thus, in Col. ii. 15, "having put off from Himself the principalities and the powers, He made a show of them openly, triumphing over them in it (the cross)." Martin Dibelius, who makes a thorough examination of this subject in his book *Die Geister-welt im Glauben des Paulus*, and maintains the genuineness of Colossians (but not of Ephesians), can show good grounds for the assertion that this theme of Colossians finds abundant parallels in the central epistles. Such passages as the following: Christ shall at last deliver up the kingdom of the Father, "when He shall have abolished all rule and all authority and power," and "put all His enemies under His feet" (1 Cor. xv. 24 f.); "that at the Name of Jesus every knee should bow" of things in heaven and in earth and under the earth (Phil. ii. 10); "who shall separate us from the love of Christ? . . . I am persuaded that neither life, nor death, nor angels, nor principalities, nor things present, nor things to come, nor height, nor depth, nor any other creature, shall be able to separate us from the love of God which is in Christ Jesus our Lord" (Rom. viii. 35 f.)—such passages show plainly that this theme is not accidental in Paul, for it recurs just in the passages where he is dwelling on the most central point of all, the love of God in Christ. It also further emphasises the objective character of the work of redemption, and its universality; the redemption affects the whole cosmos.

We may note in passing that the triumph of Christ over the demonic powers continues to be a favourite theme of the sub-apostolic writers; in particular the Apologists continually refer to it. But from the latter half of the second century onwards the demonic powers drop into the background, and their place is taken by the devil, who, as we have seen, occupies a central place in the patristic expositions.

We have seen how essential to Paul's thought is the triumph of Christ over the hostile powers. It is not that they are as yet wholly annihilated; he looks to "the end," when all power shall be taken from "His enemies" (1 Cor. xv. 24 ff.) at the advent of the new age. Yet the decisive victory has been won already; Christ has assumed His power and reigns till at last all His enemies are subjected to Him. His victory avails for all mankind: He is the Head of the new spiritual humanity. As through Adam sin entered into the world, and death through sin, so through the Second Adam comes deliverance from sin's power and newness of life. We are dead with Christ, we are risen with Christ: He died for all, and rose again; "He was delivered up for our trespasses, and was raised for our justification" (Rom. iv. 25). His work is for our sake, and it has vicarious efficacy.

It is important, above all, at this point to see clearly that this work of salvation and deliverance is at the same time a work of atonement, of reconciliation between God and the world. It is altogether misleading to say that the triumph of Christ over the powers of evil, whereby He delivers man, is a work of salvation but not of atonement; for the two ideas cannot possibly be thus separated. It is precisely the work of salvation wherein Christ breaks the power of evil that *constitutes* the atonement between God and the world; for it is by it that He removes the enmity, takes away the judgment which rested on the human race, and reconciles the world to Himself, not imputing to them their trespasses (2 Cor. v. 18). If it was right to maintain with reference to Irenæus and the other Fathers that in their teaching salvation and atonement were one and the same thing, it is still more deeply and thoroughly true of the teaching of Paul. The double aspect which is inherent in the classic idea of atonement is expressed by him more trenchantly than by them, in his view of the Law as on the one hand holy and good, and on the other as a power which held mankind in bondage. It is therefore more abundantly clear that the Pauline doctrine of salvation is also a doctrine of atonement: God through Christ saves mankind from His own judgment and His own Law, establishing a new relation which transcends the order of merit and of justice.

This central thought, that God Himself has in Christ effected both salvation and atonement, provides the key to all the passages which speak of Christ's work as vicarious, "for our sake," or "in our stead"; and all the passages which speak of "the new covenant in Christ's blood" (1 Cor. xi. 25), the "communion of the blood of Christ" (1 Cor. x. 16), of justification by the blood of Christ (Rom. v. 9), of Christ as "our Passover sacrificed for us" (1 Cor. v. 7), and so on. The Pauline use of the idea of Sacrifice lies wholly within the limits of the classic idea; note that, as Schmitz says,[3] Paul uses sacrificial imagery as freely when he speaks of his own self-oblation as Christ's apostle as when he speaks of Christ's death.

All these passages, then, which appeared to the orthodox theologians of the seventeenth century, and to many later writers, as unquestionably involving the satisfaction-theory of the Atonement, in reality belong to a quite different line of thought. Even the crucial passage, Rom. iii. 24 f. ("whom God set forth to be a propitiation, through faith, by His blood"), cannot rightly be taken to support the Latin doctrine of the Atonement;[4] for the essential point is missing, which is the special characteristic of the Latin doctrine—namely, the idea that the Divine justice was to receive adequate satisfaction for man's default, through the payment made by Christ on man's behalf. According to that doctrine the offering is made to God from man's side, from below; in Paul it is the Divine Love itself that makes the redemption.

[3] Otto Schmitz, Die Opferanschauungen des späteren Judentums und die Opferaussagen des Neuen Testaments, pp. 213 ff.

[4] Schmitz, pp. 220 ff. Cf. Wrede, Paulus, who says that while this passage leaves room for various interpretations, it contains nothing inconsistent with the fundamental Pauline thought, that "it is God's own Love itself that, the enmity being ended, brings to pass atonement and peace" (p. 78).

The classic idea of the Atonement has never found more pregnant expression than in the great passage, 2 Cor. v. 18 *f*.: "All things are of God, who reconciled us to Himself through Christ, and gave unto us the ministry of reconciliation; to wit, that God was in Christ reconciling the world unto Himself, not reckoning unto them their trespasses, and having committed unto us the word of reconciliation."

3. THE CLASSIC IDEA OF THE ATONEMENT IN THE REMAINDER OF THE NEW TESTAMENT

The limits of this work forbid more than the briefest possible sketch of the New Testament data in general.

In the Synoptic tradition we meet the image of Ransom, so dear to the Fathers: "the Son of Man is come . . . to give His life a ransom for many" (Mark x. 45)—that is to say, in order to restore men to freedom. The idea recurs often in the New Testament: "In whom we have our redemption through His blood" (Eph. i. 7); "Who gave Himself a ransom for all" (1 Tim. ii. 6); "He entered in once into the holy place, having obtained eternal redemption" (Heb. ix. 12); "ye were redeemed, not with . . . silver or gold . . . but with precious blood, as of a lamb without blemish" (1 Pet. i. 18); "that loosed us from our sins by His blood" (Rev. i. 5); and in the sub-apostolic literature, "The Lord Jesus, who was prepared beforehand thereunto, that appearing in person He might redeem out of darkness our hearts, which had already been paid over to death and delivered up to the iniquity of error" (Barnabas xiv. 5). Other variations of the idea of Christ's conflict and triumph appear in 2 Tim. i. 10: "Who abolished death, and brought life and incorruption to light"; compare "He Himself endured, that he might destroy death and show forth the resurrection of the dead" (Barnabas v. 6), and Tit. ii. 14: "Who gave Himself for us, that He might redeem us from all iniquity," and purify unto Himself a people for His own possession," and Acts xx. 28: "to feed the church of God, which He purchased with His own blood." This last text is interesting, because the redemption is directly attributed to God Himself.

In the Book of the Revelation Christ is depicted as the Lamb and as the Lion; both these images reflect the idea of conflict and triumph. "The Lion that is of the tribe of Judah . . . hath overcome" (v. 5); "Worthy is the Lamb that hath been slain to receive power"; the thought is well illustrated by the traditional symbol of the Lamb and Flag. Similarly, the Epistle to the Hebrews, in a passage which is perhaps more often quoted by the Fathers than any other New Testament text (ii. 14): "Since then the children are sharers in flesh and blood, He also Himself in like manner partook of the same; that through death He might bring to nought him that had the power of death, that is, the devil, and deliver them who through fear of death were all their lifetime subject to bondage."

The dualistic outlook is particularly prominent in the Johannine writings, with their constant antitheses, such as light and darkness, life and death. The 'world' stands over against God as a dark, hostile power: "the whole world lieth in the evil one" (1 John v. 19). Into this world Christ comes, to thrust back the evil power, to dethrone the devil: "Now is the judgment of this world; now shall the prince of this world be cast out" (John xii. 31). The way that leads Him to death leads also to glory; "the hour is come that the Son of Man should be glorified" (John xii. 23). The promised Paraclete shall convict the world, bring home to its conscience the truth about Christ's righteousness—His heavenly glory—and about judgment, "because the prince of this world hath been judged" (John xvi. 8 *ff.*); this difficult passage at any rate contains the thought of Christ's triumph through death.[5] The purpose of Christ's coming is thus summed up in 1 John iii. 8: "To this end was the Son of God manifested, that He might destroy the works of the devil."

But did the idea of conflict and triumph find expression in the words of Jesus Himself? In our day, critical exegesis is very shy of dogmatising on the question how much in the Gospel tradition can be traced back to Jesus Himself. 'Lives of Jesus' are no longer issued with the assurance that characterised the nineteenth century. But it is not only that really uncritical assurance that has passed away. When a sketch is now given to us of some part of the life and teaching of the historical Jesus, it is a very different picture from that which was commonly given in the last century. Then it was usual to set Jesus and Paul in sharp antithesis; Paul's gloomy view of mankind and the world, and his preoccupation with thoughts of salvation and redemption, were contrasted with the joyous faith of Jesus, His glad trust in God the Father, and His no less optimistic faith in men. Very little of this legend is now left; it has been banished by the discovery on the one hand of the fundamental importance of the eschatological outlook, on the other of the dualistic idea. It is with the latter that we are now concerned.

Professor Anton Fridrichsen of Uppsala has recently raised this question in an article on "The Conflict of Jesus with the Unclean Spirits."[6] Starting from a discussion of the

[5] Cf. A. Fridrichsen, "The Conflict of Jesus with the Unclean Spirits," in *Theology*, March, 1931, p. 133: "The idea of resurrection and exaltation does not—so it seems—fall directly in with the idea of the λύτρον; it is death and Sheol that form the scene of the redemption. And it is probably the oldest interpretation of Jesus' death that the death is the victory; the resurrection (glorification) comes as the reward, the seal, the completion, the manifestation of the result."

[6] In *Svensk teologisk Kvartalskrift*, Häfte 4, 1929: English translation in *Theology*, March, 1931.

exorcisms of Jesus, and the accusation that He was in league with Satan (Mark iii. 22 *ff.*), Fridrichsen shows that He rejected the popular animistic view of the demons, and regarded them all as subject to Satan, so that each exorcism was a trial of strength with Satan himself. For Jesus Satan was 'the strong one,' and the human world was his 'house.' "Jesus actualised Satan, just as He actualised God. Just as He treated with full earnest the coming Divine Kingdom, so He treated also the present dominion of Satan." He was conscious that He Himself was stronger than Satan; He had already prevailed over him. But the final end of evil would only come at the Parousia, and the intermediate period was marked by an increased activity of the hostile power, the signs of which were seen in the lack of receptivity on the part of the people and the growing hostility of their leaders. "It would seem to be incontrovertible that behind this hostility Jesus saw the great Adversary, and that this conviction shaped His thoughts of His coming death. It took the form of the realisation both that His death was inevitable and that it would mean deliverance and victory; Satan's triumph would be his undoing." "This strange paradox, that He who was stronger than Satan should succumb to the power of evil and thereby break it—this paradox was involved in His situation as the Son of Man in lowliness, but having His high vocation, and all the while an instrument of God's will." It is in this light that Fridrichsen interprets the saying that the Son of Man is come to give His life a ransom for many. Thus, so far as it is possible for us to get back to the actual outlook of Jesus on His life-work, it is seen to be altogether involved with the idea of conflict and victory.

A word more must be added on the idea of Sacrifice in the Epistle to the Hebrews; for this epistle has commonly been appealed to by the partisans of the Latin doctrine of the Atonement in support of their view. But in reality the Epistle to the Hebrews presents just the same double aspect which we have noted both in the Pauline and in the patristic teaching, as regularly characteristic of the classic idea; for it regards the Sacrifice of Christ both as God's own act of sacrifice and as a sacrifice offered to God. This double-sidedness is always alien to the Latin type, which develops the latter aspect, and eliminates the former.

The Sacrifice of Christ is primarily and above all a heavenly and "eternal" sacrifice; on this ground it supersedes the old sacrificial system. The heavenly High-priest, as R. Gyllenberg writes, "represents the heavenly world in relation to men, not men in relation to heaven; and in His work He represents God towards men, not men towards God."[7] Gyllenberg illustrates this by viii. 6, and refers also to ix. 15 *ff.*: if a testament is to be valid, the testator must die; but in this case the author of the testament is God Himself, and hence Christ dies, as it were in God's name. In any case, "Christ's incarnation and death are foreordained by God, as the expression of God's own activity, or, to use the sacrificial analogy, a sacrifice made by God Himself."[8] No earthly sacrifice made by man could effect that which is here effected; only a heavenly, divine, eternal sacrifice.

On the other hand, the writer speaks of the sacrifice as made *to* God: Christ "through the eternal Spirit offered Himself without blemish to God" (ix. 14); and Christ presents men to God as cleansed and hallowed by His Sacrifice.

We cannot go further here into the difficult argument of this epistle; but we have said enough, perhaps, to show that we have here yet one more instance of the same double-sidedness which belongs to the classic idea of the Atonement. The Sacrifice of Christ is not made part of a legal scheme, as is the case when the sacrificial idea is used in the

7 R. Gyllenberg, *Kristusbilden i Hebreerbrevet*, p. 57.
8 *Ibid.*, pp. 84 *f.*

Latin doctrine of the Atonement. To quote Gyllenberg again: "Men are called to be partakers of the heavenly, eternal world; but there is no way leading thither from earthly existence. No religion starting from man's side, no man-made sacrificial offering, can raise men to heaven. The Law cannot make perfect (Heb. vii. 19): Law cannot give salvation. In these circumstances the heavenly priesthood of Christ opens up entirely new possibilities."[9]

4. SUMMARY OF THE NEW TESTAMENT DATA

The plan of this work has not allowed of more than a rapid sketch of the New Testament data. But our survey has been sufficient to indicate that the a priori anticipation with which we began is justified by the facts, and that the New Testament teaching corresponds with that of the early church; it being understood that there is not to be found in either case a developed theological doctrine of the Atonement, but rather an idea or *motif* expressed with many variations of outward form. On the other hand, we have gathered that the New Testament does not reflect the special features of the Latin doctrine of the Atonement. This also might have been anticipated, if it is true, as we shall see in the next chapter, that the Latin doctrine gradually grew up in Western Christendom on a quite different basis—namely, the typically Latin idea of penance.

But, it may be asked, why should not a priori anticipation be allowed to tell also in the other direction? Might it not have been expected that the Latin type of view would be found in the New Testament, on the ground that the Old Testament is the basis of the New? The old orthodoxy went largely to the Old Testament for the proof-texts for its theory of the Atonement; might it not, then, be anticipated

---

[9] R. Gyllenberg, *Kristusbilden i Hebreerbrevet*, p. 60.

that the New Testament also would contain essentially the same ideas?

There is no doubt that there is plenty in the Old Testament that could serve as a basis for the Latin type of view; some (but not all) of the ideas connected with sacrifice, and, in a still greater degree, a conception of God's relation to man in which Law is the dominating factor. For in the Old Testament, in spite of strong tendencies in the opposite direction, even the idea of the Divine 'mercy' and 'grace' stands on a legalistic basis. It is Law—the Law—that says the final and decisive word in the Old Testament view of man's relation to God. Man's way to God is first and last the way of duty, of obedience to Law; and this in increasing degree as time goes on.

It is, however, exactly at this point that the emergence of the classic idea of redemption in the New Testament shows how radical the breach between Judaism and Christianity is. It must, indeed, be admitted that the classic idea of the Atonement finds anticipations in some of the greatest passages of the Old Testament, such as the image of the Divine Warrior in Isa. lix. 16 ff., and the Good Shepherd in Ezek. xxxiv. 11 ff.; nevertheless, the New Testament idea of redemption constitutes in fact a veritable revolution; for it declares that sovereign Divine Love has taken the initiative, broken through the order of justice and merit, triumphed over the powers of evil, and created a new relation between the world and God. We have seen enough in our brief survey to get some idea of the strength with which this conception dominates Apostolic Christianity. Indeed, we have the right to say that the real problem is that men have ever attempted to find in the New Testament the Latin doctrine of the Atonement; and that the only explanation is the fact that for the time being the classic idea of the Atonement had dropped clean out of sight, so that theologians had no conception of the possibility of any other idea of the Atonement than the so-called 'objective' doctrine on the one hand and the so-called 'subjective' view on the other.

5

THE MIDDLE AGES

1. BEGINNINGS OF THE LATIN THEORY OF
THE ATONEMENT

IT IS possible to fix with precision the time of the first appearance of the Latin theory. Tertullian prepares the building materials; Cyprian begins to construct out of them a doctrine of the Atonement.

In Tertullian we find the fundamental conceptions of *satisfaction* and *merit:*[1] both words apply to penance. Satisfaction is the compensation which a man makes for his fault. "How absurd it is," writes Tertullian, "to leave the penance unperformed, and yet expect forgiveness of sins! What is it but to fail to pay the price, and, nevertheless, to stretch out the hand for the benefit? The Lord has ordained that forgiveness is to be granted for this price: He wills that the remission of the penalty is to be purchased for the payment which penance makes."[2] Thus Penance is satisfaction, the acceptance of a temporal penalty to escape eternal loss. The idea of Merit is associated with the performance of that which is commanded, the observance of Law; and if such observance in general is 'meritorious,' in its special sense the

[1] *Cf.* James Morgan, *The Importance of Tertullian,* for the influence of legal conceptions on Tertullian's mind.
[2] *De Pœnitentia,* 6.

81

term is applied to acts which are 'supererogatoria,' going
beyond what is strictly of obligation; this covers, according
to Tertullian, fasting, voluntary celibacy, martyrdom, and
so forth. It is possible, therefore, for men to earn an overplus of merit.

The idea that such superfluous merit can be transferred
from one person to another is not found in Tertullian; but
it comes in Cyprian, and the way is now prepared for the
Latin theory of the Atonement. Cyprian himself begins to
apply the principle to the overplus of merit earned by Christ,
and to interpret His work as a satisfaction. He asserts that
the performance of penance can claim recognition from the
Divine justice. "Since God as Judge watches over the exercise and maintenance of justice, which is for Him the
greatest care of all, and since He regulates His government
with a view to justice, how can there be any room for doubt
that, as in general with reference to all our acts, so also here
with reference to repentance, God must act according to
justice?"[8] This point of view, of a legal relationship between
two parties, is now used to interpret the work of Christ; by
His passion and death He earns an excess of merit, and this
is paid to God as satisfaction or compensation. We have then
here the whole essence of the Latin idea of the Atonement.

It must be strongly emphasised that it was on the basis of
the penitential system that the Latin theory grew up. The
suggestion sometimes made, that the origin of Anselm's doctrine is to be found in Germanic Law, is either beside the
mark or flatly incorrect. The Latin idea of penance provides
the sufficient explanation of the Latin doctrine of the Atonement. Its root idea is that man must make an offering or payment to satisfy God's justice; this is the idea that is used to
explain the work of Christ. Two points immediately emerge:

[8] *De pœnitentia*, 2.

First, that the whole idea is essentially legalistic; and second, that, in speaking of Christ's work, the emphasis is all laid on that which is done by Christ *as man* in relation to God. It is a wholly different outlook from that of the classic idea which we have hitherto been studying.

The Latin doctrine thus begins to appear quite early in the patristic period, in the Western Church; but, as we have seen, during that period it never became the dominant view in the West, but was only gradually working its way forward, not without opposition. But for the most part it was a silent, unchallenged advance, and not seldom teaching of the Latin type can stand side by side with that of the classic type; occasionally, we even find a half-unconscious twisting of the classic type of teaching in the Latin direction. Gregory the Great, as we have seen, loved to describe the work of Christ as a conflict and triumph, with the help of the most lurid imagery; but he also sketched out the Latin idea in stronger lines than ever before, so that there is no great difference between his argument and that of the *Cur Deus homo?* He argues that human guilt necessitated a sacrifice; but no animal sacrifice could possibly be sufficient; a man must be offered for men (*ut pro rationali creatura rationalis hostia mactaretur*). The sacrifice must be undefiled; but there is no man without sin. The conclusion is that, in order that the sacrifice may be reasonable, a man must be offered, and that, in order that it may avail to cleanse men from sin, a sinless man must be offered (*ergo ut rationalis esset hostia, homo fuerat offerendus; ut vero a peccatis mundaret hominem, homo et sine peccato*). Since, therefore, there is no man who was not born of sinful seed, the Son of God is born of the Virgin and becomes man, taking on Him our nature but not our sin, and so makes the sacrifice for us. In this argument it is important to note how clearly it is stated that the sacrifice must be offered by a man on mankind's behalf; and because 'there was no other good enough to pay the price of sin,' the Son of God comes to make the offering.

2. ANSELM OF CANTERBURY

The Latin theory of the Atonement first appears fully developed in the *Cur Deus homo?* of Anselm; a book which has been so universally regarded as the typical expression of the Latin theory, that this theory has commonly been known as the Anselmian doctrine, and that the controversy on the Atonement has continually centred round Anselm's name. The assault on Protestant Orthodoxy in the seventeenth century was at the same time an assault on Anselm; on the other side he has had vigorous defenders. In the last decade, Emil Brunner has set himself to make to Anselm an act of reparation. "The working out of the idea of the expiatory punishment of sin was," he says, "an achievement of the first order"; and it seems to him no accident that the Reformers, "notably Calvin," carried on the same idea. Brunner himself wishes to follow Anselm's general line of treatment; he emphasises especially the idea of Law as the foundation on which the doctrine of Atonement must be built. "Law is the backbone, the framework, the granite-foundation of the spiritual world."[4] He criticises severely the Ritschlian condemnation of Anselm; it starts from a 'subjectivist' point of view, and fails to understand the real point.

Another modern study of Anselm, partly similar, but more thorough, will bring us straight to the central problem. R. Hermann has maintained that in Anselm's view the work of Christ is not really regarded as directed to God as its object.[5] He argues that the close association in Anselm of the

[4] "Das Gesetz ist das Rückgrat, das Knochengerüst, das granite Grund der geistigen Welt," *Der Mittler,* p. 414.
[5] 'Anselms Lehre vom Werke Christi in ihrer bleibenden Bedeutung,' in *Zeitschrift für systematische Theologie,* 1923, pp. 376–396.

doctrine of Creation with that of Atonement shows that the order of creation needed to be restored, and this was what God did through Christ. When Anselm speaks of the merit of Christ resting on His exercise of free will, this is but a manner of describing the voluntary character of Christ's work. Anselm's main object is to reject the idea, on the one hand, of a forgiveness of sin which would be a bare remission of penalty; on the other, of an optimistic conception of man's capacity to perform all that was needed. This anti-optimistic view lies behind his insistence that men were not able to make the required satisfaction. There is no thought of a transaction with God; for God Himself takes human form in the Incarnation. Hermann quotes an argument of Anselm to the effect that the dignity of mankind requires that the work of Atonement be carried out by God Himself; were it performed by angels or by other men, then the human race would become their slaves. He finds a confirmation of his thesis that it is God Himself who thus restores His own honour, in Anselm's remark (*Cur Deus homo?*, II., 18) that the God-man offered Himself to His own glory —that is to say, His humanity was an offering to His Divine nature. If, now, this interpretation of Hermann's is right, there is evidently insufficient ground for the sharp distinction that we have made between Anselm's theory and the classic idea of the Atonement.

It is certainly true that Anselm's teaching has often been misinterpreted, and that many, or most, of the criticisms which have been levelled against it are valid only against a misrepresentation of it which amounts to a caricature. Thus it has constantly been said, especially in popular expositions, that Anselm taught that a direct change in God's attitude was effected by Christ's satisfaction; but this is not what Anselm said. But a more serious fault in the common criticism of Anselm has been the assumption that the Anselmian doctrine and the 'subjective' view are exclusive alternatives: in this respect Ritschl and Harnack were guilty of a lack of true perspective. But their critics, Brunner and Hermann, fall into the same mistake; they, too, fail to envisage the contrast of Anselm's view with the classic idea of the Atonement.

This is the decisive issue; and, therefore, the crucial question is really this: Does Anselm treat the atoning work of Christ as the work of God Himself from start to finish? Now Hermann is fully justified in pointing to the close association in Anselm of creation and Atonement; Anselm does regard the Atonement as the restoration of the impaired order of creation. It follows that God, as it were, takes the initiative in the work of Atonement, and that, therefore, it is wrong to speak of a change in God's attitude. But this point does not really touch the central question of God's part in the actual accomplishment of the atoning work.

Hermann attaches very great weight to the assertion (*Cur Deus homo?*, II., 6) that men are not able to pay the satisfaction which God requires; and he infers that, therefore, God must do all, and in fact does all. But his conclusion is too hastily drawn, and he has not grasped the essential structure of Anselm's thought. In order to understand this, it is necessary to bear in mind that the whole structure is built on the basis of the penitential system. Anselm's basic assumption is that the required satisfaction for transgression must be made by man, and the argument proceeds: Men are not able to make the necessary satisfaction, because they are all sinful. If men cannot do it, then God must do it. But, on the other hand, the satisfaction must be made by man, because man is guilty. The only solution is that God becomes man; this is the answer to the question *Cur Deus homo?*

Now the essential point comes just here: Anselm *does not,* as Hermann seems to think, *give up his basic assumption* that the required satisfaction must be made by man; on the contrary, he holds firmly to it, and the whole object of his argument is to show how the Man appears who is able to give the satisfaction which God absolutely demands. *The satisfaction must be made by man; and this is precisely what is done in Christ's atoning work.*

It is therefore essential to the theory of Anselm that the Incarnation and the Atonement are not organically connected together, as they were in the classic view. There we found a simple and straightforward connection of thought: God enters into this world of sin and death that He may overcome the enemies that hold mankind in bondage, and Himself accomplish the redemptive work, for which no power but the Divine is adequate. But for Anselm the central problem is: Where can a man be found, free from sin and guilt, and able to offer himself as an acceptable sacrifice to God? Therefore his answer to the question *Cur Deus homo?* is by no means so simple as that of Irenæus and Athanasius; indeed, he can only obtain his desired proof of the necessity of the Incarnation with the help of secondary lines of thought. One such is the argument, which he shares with earlier representatives of the Latin doctrine, that the union of the Divine nature with the human nature in Christ confers on His work a greater value than it would otherwise have; another, that it would conflict with the dignity of man if the satisfaction were made by an angel or by one who was merely human. Note the significant emphasis on the dignity of man.

All this goes to show that the doctrine of the Incarnation is no longer with him a fully living idea, as it was to the Fathers. It is a fixed dogma, which he takes for granted as beyond dispute; but his deductions only with difficulty succeed in relating it with his doctrine of Atonement. It is an inheritance from the past, which is not altogether at home in its new environment. Here, then, the contrast between Anselm and the Fathers is as plain as daylight. They show how God became incarnate that He might redeem; he teaches a human work of satisfaction, accomplished by Christ. Anselm is anxious to insist that the voluntary offering up of self even to death is the greatest sacrifice and the highest gift that man can make to God: *nihil autem asperius aut difficilius potest homo ad honorem Dei sponte et non ex debito pati, quam mortem, et nullatenus seipsum potest homo magis dare Deo, quam cum se morti tradit ad honorem illius* (*Cur Deus homo?*, II., 11). And the very words which Hermann quotes to support his interpretation really prove the exact opposite; for when Anselm throws out the idea that Christ even pays satisfaction to His own Divine nature, he is saying, as clearly as words can express, that he is thinking of that which Christ accomplishes as man, of an offering made to God from man's side, from below.

It is, indeed, true that Anselm and his successors treat the Atonement as in a sense God's work; God is the author of the plan, and He has sent His Son and ordered it so that the required satisfaction shall be made. Nevertheless, it is not in the full sense God's work of redemption. If the patristic idea of Incarnation and Redemption may be represented by a continuous line, leading obliquely downwards, the doctrine of Anselm will require a broken line; or, the line that leads downwards may be shown as crossed by a line leading from below upwards, to represent the satisfaction made to God by Christ as man. Then, too, the double-sidedness characteristic of the classic idea has disappeared. God is no longer regarded as *at once* the agent and the object of the reconciliation, but as *partly* the agent, as being the author of the plan, and *partly* the object, when the plan comes to be carried out.

The contrast symbolised by the continuous and the broken line can be studied also under two other aspects. First, the old dualistic outlook is explicitly rejected by Anselm. He violently repudiates the old idea of a ransom paid to the devil; and while it is true that he sometimes speaks of Christ's work as a triumph over the devil, and connects this thought with the idea of satisfaction, this use of the old phraseology is purely accidental. It has no vital relation to the structure of his thought; it is a mere relic of tradition, introduced among an environment which is strange to it. The clearest sign of the thoroughness with which he discards the dualistic outlook is his interpretation of the meaning of Christ's death. His whole emphasis is on the death as an isolated fact, and as in itself constituting the satisfaction; but, according to the classic type of view, the death had been the climax of a long conflict, and had constituted Christ's victory. Hence, also, the note of triumph which had always been typical of the classic idea, from the Apostolic Age onwards, is damped down. The reason is that the dualistic outlook has gone, or, what comes to the same thing, that the work of atonement is no longer seen as directly the work of God.

Secondly, if the line leading downwards is now a broken line, the order of law and justice is not allowed to be infringed; it is absolutely necessary that satisfaction be made by man to God's justice. We find in Anselm, as in every form of the Latin theory of the Atonement, the alternative stated: *either* a forgiveness of sins by God, which would mean that sin is not treated seriously and so would amount to a toleration of laxity, *or* satisfaction. No other possibility is regarded as conceivable. The vindication of the justice of God and His judgment on sin necessarily involves a making-good, a compensation, which satisfies the demands of justice. Hence the payment of satisfaction is emphasised as a safeguard of moral earnestness; and Anselm meets every attempt to challenge the absolute necessity for the satisfaction with his *nondum considerasti quanti ponderis sit peccatum*—"you have not yet fully weighed the gravity of sin."

This rigid dilemma fastens the doctrine of the Atonement into a juridical scheme. It is an indispensable necessity that God shall receive the satisfaction which alone can save forgiveness from becoming laxity; and this need is met by Christ's death. The Atonement is worked out according to the strict requirements of justice; God receives compensation for man's default. It is not, indeed, fair to charge Anselm with saying that God's attitude is changed by the satisfaction made to Him; such an imputation misses the real point, and, as we have seen, it is inconsistent with his assertion that God is the ultimate author of the scheme of Atonement. It is His will that Christ on behalf of men should make the satisfaction which His justice demands.

Thus the whole conception of Atonement is juridical in its inmost essence; and the same legal idea is carried further, when he goes on to show how the merit earned by Christ becomes available for men. The idea derived from the penitential system comes in again; it is asserted to be fully in accord with the demands of justice when the superfluous merit earned by Christ is carried to the credit of His brethren.

The juridical idea thus holds an entirely different position here from the limited place which it had held in the classic teaching. The relation of man to God is treated by Anselm as essentially a legal relation, for his whole effort is to prove that the atoning work is in accordance with justice. To use Brunner's phrase, in this scheme Law really is represented as the granite-foundation of the spiritual world. To the classic idea, on the other hand, it is essential that the work of atonement which God accomplishes in Christ reflect a Divine order which is wholly different from a legal order;

the Atonement is not accomplished by strict fulfilment of the demands of justice, but in spite of them; God is not, indeed, unrighteous, but He transcends the order of justice.

Closely connected with the juridical character of the Latin theory is its rational character. Anselm's continual refrain is *nihil rationabilius*; nothing can be more reasonable than the demand for satisfaction, and the way in which the demand is met. *Lex et ratio*, law and rationality, are, as Luther is never tired of saying, inseparable allies. But the classic idea of the Atonement defies rational systematisation; its essential double-sidedness, according to which God is at once the Reconciler and the Reconciled, constitutes an antinomy which cannot be resolved by a rational statement.

This may suffice for a summary of the contrast between the classic view of the Atonement and the Latin type, as it is represented by Anselm. It may be summed up thus: The classic idea shows a continuity in the Divine action and a discontinuity in the order of justice; the Latin type, a legal consistency and a discontinuity in Divine operation. But one more point remains.

It is often claimed that the strength of the Latin doctrine lies in the ethical seriousness which characterises it; in the emphasis which it lays on the Divine justice as contrary to sin, on men's guilt before God, and men's powerlessness to make for themselves an atonement for sin. This ethical seriousness we have already noticed in the dilemma which makes the payment of satisfaction the alternative to a lax charity. And it is certain that Anselm is anxious to avoid any such idea of the Divine Love as may minimise the gravity of sin; he claims that God's demand for satisfaction proves the seriousness with which He regards sin.

But while it is necessary to admit this intention of moral earnestness, we cannot forget that this doctrine of the Atonement grew up on a moralistic basis; and it can truly be said that the very fact that a satisfaction paid to God is regarded as making amends for man's fault shows quite decidedly that the radical opposition of God to sin has become weakened down. If God can be represented as willing to accept a satisfaction for sins committed, it appears to follow necessarily that the dilemma of laxity or satisfaction really fails to guard the truth of God's enmity against sin. The doctrine provides for the remission of the punishment due to sins, but not for the taking away of the sin itself. It may further be noted that Anselm also admits a 'non-personal' transference of Christ's merit to men, a point which so enthusiastic a champion as Brunner reckons as a fault; and, also, that when he comes to speak of penance for sins committed after Baptism, Anselm, like other Latin theologians, allows that men can earn merit in God's sight.

All this goes to show that the Latin doctrine of the Atonement is closely related to the legalism characteristic of the mediæval outlook. Therefore, it ought to appear as a really amazing fact, that the post-Reformation theologians accepted the Anselmian doctrine of the Atonement without suspicion, altogether missing the close relation between this doctrine and the theological tradition which the Reformation had challenged with its watchword of *sola gratia*. We shall return to this problem in a later chapter; for the present let it suffice to say that part of the reason was the false assumption that Luther had accepted the Anselmian theory, and the fact that the classic idea of the Atonement, as a distinct form of teaching, had practically dropped out of men's minds.

3. THE THEOLOGY OF THE LATER MIDDLE AGES

I shall not attempt to trace, even in outline, the history of the doctrine of the Atonement in the hands of the scholastic theologians. It is more important for our present purpose to call attention to certain outstanding points, which will be found to throw additional light on the true character and structure of the Latin doctrine.

The dominant view of the Atonement was, if not Anselm's system in its completeness, at least the Latin type of doctrine. The prevailing ideas may be thus summed up: The payment of satisfaction is treated as the essential element in Atonement and as accomplished by the death of Christ; the payment is primarily the work of Christ's human nature, but it gains increased meritorious value on account of the union of human nature with the Divine nature in Christ. So Thomas Aquinas teaches explicitly: the human nature of Christ makes the offering, but, because He is God, the merit of His work is not merely sufficient, but superabundant. Thus our analysis is verified; the line of the Divine operation in the work of redemption is crossed by the line which represents the offering made to God by the human nature.

It has been usual to sum up the difference between Anselm's teaching and that of the later scholastics by pointing to the fact that Thomas speaks of Christ's work of satisfaction as also including the endurance of punishment. It is, however, a mistake to lay much stress on this point; at most it is merely a difference of expression, and it involves no change in outlook. The thought of Christ as enduring vicarious punishment is indeed found in Anselm himself, though not in the *Cur Deus homo?*; but, quite apart from this, it is clear that the idea of satisfaction passes over naturally and easily into that of punishment, since the satisfaction which Christ made consisted in the vicarious endurance of a death which, if men had endured it, would have been their

punishment. Further, the idea of punishment had been expressed by Anselm's predecessors. In any case, the ideas of
penance, satisfaction, and punishment are all closely related.

Far more real and significant is the difference that Anselm's successors did not follow him in the method of strin-
gent demonstration, which is expressed in his constant formula *nihil rationabilius*. The claim of rational demonstration
which he had made was treated as a dubious novelty; and a
return was made to the older treatment of the satisfaction
made by Christ, as a congruous and fitting method of Atonement, not the necessary and only method.

From this point of view the Nominalism which marks the
final stage of scholastic theology represents the disintegration of Anselm's theory. The usual Latin ideas are repeated,
but their basis has been undermined. The Nominalist criticism is that in the last resort all depends on the arbitrary act
of God in accepting the satisfaction. The work of Christ
has no value necessarily belonging to it, but only such value
as God is pleased to recognise in it. It could not be called
necessary that mankind should make the satisfaction which
Anselm had laid down, for the sin committed by finite men
could not involve an infinite guilt. Nor, again, could the
merit of Christ be infinite, since He only suffered in His
human nature. Finally, no such infinite merit could be necessary, since God can assess any meritorious act precisely as
He pleases.

Such arguments involved the dissolution of the Latin
theory. Yet at the same time its general outline was assumed
as authoritative. For our present purpose, the point of special
interest is the argument that the merit of Christ cannot be
infinite because He only suffered in His human nature; this
criticism shows that our interpretation of the Latin doctrine
was correct, when we insisted that this doctrine had lost

sight of the older patristic teaching, that the Atonement is the work of God Himself throughout.

While, however, the Latin doctrine was altogether the dominant teaching of mediæval theology, certain reminiscences of the classic idea of the Atonement still persisted, both in the earlier and in the middle period of scholasticism. Peter Lombard, on whom, we may remember, Luther commented in his early period, reproduces in abundance the old classic imagery. The Synod of Sens in 1141 condemned certain propositions of Abelard, in which he had denied that men were delivered by Christ from the devil's dominion, and that the previous dominion of the devil over man was in accordance with justice; and here we may remark in passing that this condemnation was equally relevant to the teaching of Anselm. In Thomas, also, certain of the characteristic points of the classic view appear, such as the deliverance of men from the power of the devil, which he seeks to reconcile with the idea of satisfaction. But these are only lingering traces of the classic idea of the Atonement; the Latin view was decisively the dominant type of theory. The situation is, then, thoroughly clear and intelligible. The Latin doctrine of the Atonement was completely in accord with the general nature of mediæval theology, with its typical emphasis on penance and on the Sacrifice of the Mass. The doctrine of penance emphasised the necessity of satisfaction, and the Mass was interpreted primarily as a sacrifice for sins.

4. ABELARD

It has for a long time been a commonplace of the historical study of dogma to lay emphasis on the rivalry between Anselm and his younger contemporary Abelard, and to claim the latter as the father of the so-called 'subjective' doctrine of the Atonement. In general, these assertions are sound enough. The interesting thing about Abelard is that the Latin theory of the Atonement had no sooner received its complete theological formulation than it found a critic; it may be said that the controversy thus begun has continued ever since.

Abelard attacked the imagery of the classic idea of the Atonement and its dualistic outlook, as well as Anselm's theory. On the one hand, he refused to allow the idea of the Atonement to be connected in any way with the devil; on the other, he sought to prove the impossibility of the idea of satisfaction, for if Adam's lesser fault required such a satisfaction, how much greater ought to be the satisfaction demanded by sins against Christ! Thus he seeks to blaze a trail along a different line. He emphasises especially that Christ is the great Teacher and Example, who arouses responsive love in men; this love is the basis on which reconciliation and forgiveness rest. Here he quotes Luke vii. 47: "Much is forgiven to them that love much." This love awakened in men is treated by Abelard as meritorious; for even he cannot escape from the traditional Latin scheme of merit. But though his teaching thus bears a more 'subjective' character, since the emphasis is now laid on that which is done by men, it cannot be said that it follows this line consistently; Abelard feels compelled to assign a place to the merit of Christ, which, he says, makes complete the merit of man by the virtue of His intercession for them.

Apart from a few isolated points, it cannot be said that Abelard's thought exercised any great influence in the Middle Ages. He was, indeed, so far in accord with the mind of the period that all his thought lay on the moralistic level; but, on the whole, he was far too radically opposed to the common view to gain a hearing. In particular, the fact that he attached no special significance to the death of Christ was sufficient of itself to make his teaching unacceptable to an age which was laying ever greater stress on the death, both in theology and in devotional practice.

5. THE DEVOTIONAL ASPECT

Far more important, therefore, was the influence of the religious phenomenon of *Devotion to the Passion*, or Passion-mysticism; indeed, it would be hard to exaggerate the importance of this, either in the Middle Ages or in the subsequent period, both in Roman and in Protestant Christendom. Unfortunately, this chapter in the history of the Christian religion has never yet received a thorough investigation; this is a work which greatly needs to be undertaken. We shall attempt here only the briefest possible outline of the subject.

This Devotion to the Passion stands to mediæval theology in a double relation, of simultaneous attraction and repulsion. On the one hand, it is clear that neither the scholastic arguments based on the Divine Justice, nor the key-idea of satisfaction itself, could make any special appeal to the devout soul; on the other, theology and piety agreed in concentrating their attention on the passion and death of Christ. Here, however, there is again a difference; for while the emphasis of theology was laid on the death as such, piety directed its gaze to the passion of Christ as a whole, contemplating it as a martyrdom. It can truly be said that the appeal of the passion, the martyrdom of Christ, has never been so deeply felt as in mediæval religion: "The whole life of Christ was a cross and a martyrdom," says à Kempis in the *Imitatio Christi*. The attitude of the Christian is to be *meditatio et imitatio*; to enter with loving compassion into the unspeakable sufferings of Christ, to follow in His steps, and so be cleansed and united with the eternal Divine Love: *per vulnera humanitatis ad intima divinitatis.*

This Devotion to the Passion acted both as a complement to the Latin doctrine of the Atonement and as a counter-poise to it. It is, indeed, not surprising that an emotional mysticism of this type should appear side by side with the thoroughly rationalistic and juridical theory of the satisfaction of God's justice. Just in the same way the Pietism of Herrnhuth in the eighteenth century emerged in an age which could find no religious satisfaction in the same doctrine of the Atonement in its Protestant form, and produced the evangelical hymns of the Passion whose tone is closely similar to that of mediæval devotion.

Finally, it is to be noted that this Devotion to the Passion co-operated with the Latin theory in banishing what remained of the classic idea of the Atonement; perhaps, rather, that piety effectively completed the work that theology had begun. What was lost was the note of triumph, which is as much absent in the contemplation of the Sacred Wounds as in the theory of the satisfaction of God's justice. This is reflected very significantly in later mediæval art. The triumph-crucifix of an earlier period is now ousted by the crucifix which depicts the human Sufferer.

6. THE CLASSIC IDEA OF THE ATONEMENT IN THE MIDDLE AGES

Yet it would be wrong to infer that the classic idea of the Atonement had been wholly lost. It was far too deep-rooted and powerful to disappear altogether; and it still lived on in hymnody and in art.

In hymns and sequences we meet again and again the old language of the Divine conflict and victory, and even sometimes the old realistic imagery. Above all is this true of the Easter liturgy; for the Easter festival has always been the central stronghold of the classic view of the Atonement. A well-known instance is the Easter sequence, which the

Roman missal has retained, *Victimæ paschali*,[6] which sets forth the conflict of Life with Death and the triumph of the Prince of Life. Other examples may be found in Adam of St. Victor, Ezzo, and Honorius Augustodunensis. But this is another subject which still awaits adequate investigation.

We might also point to the occurrence of the dramatic idea in the mystery plays, with the *caveat* that here the devil gradually becomes a half-comical figure; for the idea of the conflict of Christ with the devil was no longer taken seriously. But the frequency of the occurrence of the dramatic idea in sacred poetry shows that it was still alive in the consciousness of Christendom, even though it had been all but suppressed in theology.

We have already alluded to the disappearance of the triumph-crucifix in sacred art. But, even if this type was ousted by the other, we must not forget that the crucifixes of the older type date from the finest period of mediæval art, and that they portray exactly the classic idea of the Atonement. They show Christ as at once the Sufferer and the Victor who gains His triumph by the sacrifice of Himself. It is further to be remembered that these works both of poetry and art, which date from before the fourteenth century, remained in existence in the later period to bear their witness to the idea of redemption which they expressed.

These few notes on an important subject may suffice to show that the classic idea of the Atonement was never quite lost in the Middle Ages. Other currents, of theology and of devotion, ran strongly on the surface; but, deep below, the current from early Christianity still continued to flow. Poetry and art remained to testify to the power which it still exerted on men's minds; it emerged also in preaching. Even in the latest period of the Middle Ages it was not quite dead;

---

[6] E. T. in *English Hymnal*, No. 130. For other instances belonging to this period see Hymns 122 and 129.

and when it came to the surface, with greater power than ever before, in Martin Luther, it could appeal not only to Apostolic and patristic tradition, but to a faith that still lived in men's hearts.

6

LUTHER

IT MAY be roundly stated that no side of Luther's theology has been more summarily treated or more grossly misinterpreted than his teaching on the Atonement. The fundamental mistake has been the assumption that his teaching on this subject belongs to the Anselmian type.

Certainly it was impossible to fail to perceive that Luther continually presents us with thoughts about Christ's work which cannot be fitted into the scheme of the scholastic doctrine; but these have usually been treated, either as relatively unimportant, or as having nothing to do with 'Atonement' properly so called. Theodosius Harnack, the author of the most thorough treatment of Luther in the latter half of the nineteenth century, notices how often Luther returns to the thought of Christ's work as a victory over the 'tyrants'; but he treats such utterances as concerned only with salvation and not with atonement, and, in regard to the latter, he regards Luther's theology as belonging to the Latin type. A. Ritschl notes the occurrence of the dramatic outlook again and again in Luther, but he dismisses it summarily as "no improvement on the mediæval doctrine"; Luther's teaching on the Atonement belongs to the same 'juridical' type as Anselm's, and hence his theology as a whole suffers from an unreconciled antinomy between his teaching on Justification, which stands in sharp contrast with mediæval moralism, and his atonement-doctrine, which still maintains the idea of merit that elsewhere he has overcome. In this case there is a continuity of tradition between Anselm, Luther, and Lutheran Orthodoxy.

The same general view of the matter has been continued in Ritschl's successors. It is repeated even in R. Otto's essay on the numinous element in Luther,[1] and also in E. Brunner, who describes the *Strafsühngedanke*, the idea of the expiatory punishment of sin, as worked out by Anselm, and also finding full expression in the Reformers; he adds, however, that it was Calvin who took the chief share in this work.[2] K. Holl and his followers have taken a somewhat different attitude; but even they have not fully grasped the true character of Luther's teaching, and his revival of the classic idea of the Atonement, because they have not made a special investigation of this type of atonement-doctrine.

I shall now maintain that Luther's teaching can only be rightly understood as a revival of the old classic theme of the Atonement as taught by the Fathers, but with a greater depth of treatment.[3]

[1] *Aufsätze das Numinose betreffend*, p. 200.

[2] *Der Mittler*, pp. 413 f.

[3] The reasons which explain what must, in my view, appear as an amazing misinterpretation of Luther's teaching, may be summed up as three; they will all be fully illustrated in this chapter and the next. (1) The doctrine of the Atonement was not raised in Luther's day as a polemical issue, and thus his utterances on the subject attracted relatively little attention. (2) Luther's use, in a new sense, of such typically 'Latin' terms as Satisfaction and Merit was not unnaturally misunderstood. (3) There has been a general assumption that the so-called 'objective' and 'subjective' views of the Atonement are exclusive alternatives; the existence of the classic idea has been all but overlooked, and its typical features have not been noticed.

I would like to add here a warm appreciation of a book on Luther which has lately appeared in Sweden: *Dualismen hos Luther*, by Ragnar

2. THE CLASSIC IDEA OF THE ATONEMENT IN LUTHER

The decisive proof that Luther's teaching on the Atonement belongs to the classic type is not merely that he uses images and forms of expression which are regularly characteristic of the classic idea of the Atonement; for the same is true, though in a less degree, of the great scholastics. Nor is it even that we constantly and regularly find in Luther the dramatic view of the work of Christ and its meaning as a Divine conflict and victory. Luther loves violent expressions, strong colours, realistic images, and in innumerable passages he describes Christ's conflict with the tyrants in this way. For him no colours are too strong, no images too concrete; even the most grotesque analogies from the Fathers come back again. They had been discarded by scholasticism, in proud consciousness of having found a purer and more rational explanation; but now they all return. Luther seems to have a special fondness for the grossest symbols of all, especially that of the deception of the devil. To take one example among many,[4] he describes how it was the Lord of glory, not a mere man, who was crucified; but God concealed this fact from the devil, or he would never have dared assail Him. God acts like a fisherman, who binds a line to a fishing-rod, attaches a sharp hook, fixes on it a worm, and casts it into the water. The fish comes, sees the worm but not the hook, and bites, thinking that he has taken a good morsel; but the hook is fixed firm in his gills and he is caught. So God does; Christ must become man; God sends Him from high heaven into the world, where the devil finds Him

---

Bring. This book is carefully documented, and fixes with precision what Luther actually said on the subject; it has the further merit of interpreting Luther's teaching on the Atonement in relation to his teaching as a whole.

[4] Luther's *Works* (Weimar edn.), XX., pp. 334 *f.*

like "a worm and no man" (Ps. xxii. 6), and swallows Him up. But this is to him as food which he cannot digest. "For Christ sticks in his gills, and he must spue Him out again, as the whale the prophet Jonah, and even as he chews Him the devil chokes himself and is slain, and is taken captive by Christ." So the word of Hosea is fulfilled: "I will ransom them from hell; I will redeem them from death: O Death, I will be thy plague; O Hell, I will be thy destruction." Such realistic passages could be quoted by the score; and the fact that Luther so constantly returns to the theme of Christ's victory over the tyrants proves that it can be no accident.

Yet the decisive proof of the real character of Luther's teaching on the Atonement is not to be found even in the fact that he so frequently uses such imagery, but rather is to be summed up in the following three points:

First, in those places where it is altogether necessary for him to express himself with the greatest possible care and the greatest possible exactness, as, for instance, in the Catechisms, he always returns to the dramatic idea.

Second, he himself repeatedly assures us, with all possible clearness, that the statements of the meaning of the Atonement in dramatic terms give the very essence of the Christian faith; they are *capitalia nostræ theologiæ*.

Third, and chiefly, the dramatic view of the work of Christ stands in organic relation with his theological outlook as a whole.

In the *Lesser Catechism* the crucial words describing the work of Christ are as follows: "He has delivered, purchased, and won me, a lost and doomed man, from all sins, from death and the devil's power." It is strange to reflect on the numberless attempts which have been made for centuries past to twist these words round so as to read into them the Latin doctrine of the Atonement. For it is as plain as daylight that the idea which they embody is identical with that of the Fathers; the three enemies here mentioned are just the familiar trio of the early church: sin, death, and the devil. It can be no accident that Luther expresses himself thus; for we know with what extraordinary care he weighed every word in the *Lesser Catechism*. Any doubts that remain are dispelled by the *Greater Catechism*. On the Christological section of the Creed, Luther says that the whole Gospel means that we must grasp this part of the Creed as that on which our whole salvation is based. The whole weight rests, he says, on the word *Lord*: Christ as our Lord. "What is it now to be a 'Lord'? It is this, that He has redeemed me from sin, from the devil, from death and all woe. For before, I had not yet had any Lord, nor King, but had been held captive under the devil's power, doomed to death, ensnared in sin and blindness. . . . Now, therefore, those tyrants and gaolers are all crushed, and in their place is come Jesus Christ, a Lord of Life, righteousness, all good and holiness, and He has snatched us poor lost men from the jaws of hell, won us, made us free, and brought us back to the Father's goodness and grace."[5]

It is further most illuminative that Luther's most powerful and most characteristic hymns are built up on the same theme; such as *Nun freut euch lieben Christen gmein* and *Ein feste Burg*.

I will quote just one more typical passage; it is perhaps the passage which of all others most exactly sets forth the central points on which Luther's whole teaching depends. It is taken from the *Longer Commentary on Galatians*:[6] "Thus the curse, which is the wrath of God against the whole world, was in conflict with the blessing—that is to say, with

[5] Luther's *Works*, XXX., i., p. 186.
[6] On Gal. iii. 13: "Christ redeemed us from the curse of the Law, having become a curse for us . . . that upon the Gentiles might come the blessing of Abraham in Christ Jesus."

God's eternal grace and mercy in Christ. The curse conflicts with the blessing, and would condemn it and altogether annihilate it, but it cannot. For the blessing is divine and eternal, therefore the curse must yield. For if the blessing in Christ could yield, then God Himself would have been overcome. But that is impossible. Christ, who is God's power, righteousness, blessing, grace, and life, overcomes and carries away these monsters, sin, death, and the curse." (Here he quotes Col. ii. 15: "Having put off from Himself the principalities and the powers, He made a show of them openly, triumphing over them in it.") "When therefore thou lookest upon this person thou seest sin, death, God's wrath, hell, the devil, and all evil, overcome and dead. In so far therefore as Christ by His grace rules in the hearts of the faithful, there is found no more sin, death, and curse; but where Christ is not known they still remain. Thus they that believe not lack this benefit and this victory. For our victory, as John says, is our faith. This is the primary article of Christian teaching, which in time past sophists hid in darkness, and which fanatics now obscure.[7] And here thou seest how necessary it is to believe and to confess the article about Christ's Deity. When Arius denied this he must also deny *articulum redemptionis.* For, by Himself to overcome the world's sin, death, the curse, and God's wrath, this is not the work of any created being, but of almighty God. Therefore He who of Himself overcame these must actually in His nature be God. For against these so mighty powers, sin, death, and the curse, which of themselves have dominion in the world and in all creation, another and a higher power must appear, which can be none other than God. To destroy sin, to smite death, to take away the curse by Himself, to bestow righteousness, bring life to light, and give the blessing: to annihilate the

---

[7] The *Shorter Commentary on Galatians* (1531) reads here: "Ista sunt capitalia nostræ theologiæ, quæ obscuraverunt Sophistæ."

former, and to create the latter: this is the work of God's omnipotence alone. But when the Scripture ascribes to Christ all this, then is He Himself the Life, and Righteousness, and Blessing—that is, in His nature and His essence He is God. Therefore those who deny Christ's Deity lose all Christianity and become mere heathens and Turks. Therefore the article of Justification must, as I am continually saying, be exactly understood. For in this all the other articles of our faith are included, and if this remain whole then all the others remain whole. When therefore we teach that men are justified through Christ, and Christ is the conqueror of sin, death, and the everlasting curse, then at the same time we testify that He is in His nature God."

These words might be taken as a text on which to hang an exposition of the whole essence of Lutheran theology. He is speaking of that which lies nearest to his heart, and he does it in language which cannot be misunderstood. Two things are perfectly clear: First, that we are again listening to the classic idea of the Atonement—indeed, we get the impression that it is being presented with a greater intensity and power than ever before; and, second, that the dramatic view of the work of Christ, which Luther so emphatically expresses, is organically and inseparably connected with his doctrine of Justification. That we are justified through Christ is, he says, one and the same thing as to say that He is the conqueror of sin, death, and the everlasting curse. Likewise we hear that this is the very centre of the Christian faith (*capitalia nostræ theologiæ*).

Luther's interpretation of Christ's work has all the typical characteristics of the classic idea of the Atonement. First, there is here a continuity of Divine operation. Time after time Luther returns to this theme and emphasises it with all his might: the one power which is able to overcome the tyrants is God's omnipotence. If the tyrants were victorious, then were God Himself overcome. But now almighty God Himself steps in and carries through His work to victory.

Second, the Atonement is once again closely connected with the Incarnation. You see, he says, how necessary it is to confess the article about Christ's Deity. All depends on the Incarnation; there is no thought of an offering made to God by Christ simply as man, in His human nature. It is clear, therefore, how radically false is that interpretation of Luther which maintains that he laid all the emphasis on that which is purely human in Christ, or on the historical Jesus, and that the patristic Christology is retained by him only as a tolerated survival. All depends on the assertion that it is God Himself who in Christ overcomes the tyrants. It is at the same time evident that the Deity of Christ is not for Luther a bare metaphysical dogma, still less a 'physical' doctrine; for in the work of redemption the actual agent is no other and no less than God's own Blessing, Righteousness, and Life.

Third, the whole view is dualistic and dramatic. The description is of a stupendous conflict, a *mirabile duellum*, in which Christ prevails. Once again, therefore, we hear the note of triumph which rang through the early church. The atmosphere has changed from that of mediæval scholasticism and mediæval devotion to the Passion. We have only to listen to Luther's hymns to feel how they thrill with triumph, like a fanfare of trumpets.

There should, then, be no doubt at all that in Luther we meet again the classic idea of the Atonement. It is the patristic view that has returned; but it has returned with greater depth and force than before. We may see this most clearly in his treatment of the enemies from which Christ delivers mankind. He enumerates a long series of these; the names are partly synonyms, and they can be brought down to five: sin, death, the devil, law, and the wrath. To the regular trio of the Fathers he adds two. In counting Law as a 'tyrant' he is picking up the Pauline teaching; but the inclusion of Wrath—that is to say, the Wrath of God—calls for special attention, and we shall return to it in a little while to study it carefully. But it is necessary first to deal briefly with Luther's use of imagery.

We have seen how Luther loves to paint with strong colours and seems to have a special liking for the most realistic imagery of the Fathers. It is therefore the more important to see how clearly he understands and explains that such images are only images. He distinguishes explicitly between the idea itself and the imagery in which it is clothed; yet the use of images is not superfluous, for it is by images that these matters are best set forth. He has some very significant words in a passage where he is expounding the Descent into hell. If, he says, one were to speak acutely and cleverly of the subject as it is in itself, even so one would never thoroughly explain the truth of the matter; but by using imagery one can describe how Christ went down with banner in hand, and smote the devils and chased them away, and stormed hell's citadel. It would now be easy to ask, with a smile, what sort of a banner He had when He took hell's castle, and what it was made of, and why it was not burnt up in hell's fire, or what sort of a gate there could be in hell, and so to ridicule as simpletons the Christians who believed such things. But this would be a fool's game, such as a swine or a cow might join in! So one might make allegories of it and explain what the banner, the pole, the flag, and the gate of hell signify. Christians could hardly be so coarse as to believe or say that it happened so in outward appearance, or that hell were a structure of wood or iron; rather, they left such speculations on one side and spoke in a simple way of such things, just as always the doctrine of Divine things is set forth in crude outward images;

as also Christ used images and parables in speaking of the mysteries of the Kingdom of Heaven.[8]

In this connection we may return to Luther's idea of the devil and his constant descriptions of the deception of the devil. The continual alternation of the mention of the devil with that of the other enemies—sin, death, law, and wrath—shows that his idea of the devil is not a mere piece of mythology, but that he is thinking rather of a power of evil really existing in the world of men, and of the devil as a sort of embodiment of this evil power. Certainly the war against the devil is fought out on the human stage and is identical with the war against the other 'tyrants.'

. His frequent use of the idea of the deception of the devil is closely connected with an important element in his theology, the thought of the Hidden God (*Deus absconditus*). Luther returns to this theme in a number of places, and the term varies somewhat in meaning, as I have sought to show elsewhere.[9] But one side of his meaning is that the Revealed God (*Deus revelatus*) meets us in the world as a Hidden God; God was present, hidden, in the despised man Christ, in His lowliness, and in His self-devotion to suffering and to death. This is the idea that underlies the image of the devil's deception. In Him the mightiest of all powers was present, hidden; but the 'enemies' did not understand this fact when they assailed Him. Hence the language about the devil's deception is the expression of a very deep thought of Luther, that *Deus revelatus* is always at the same time *Deus absconditus*; the God who reveals Himself and delivers man is also present, hidden, in the lowliest and most despised. This is God's 'deceit'; and the idea is in essence closely related to that which Luther develops when he shows how even that which is good in itself can have the effect of hardening, and

[8] Luther's *Works* (Weimar edn.), XXXVII., p. 63; Bring, pp. 129 *ff.*
[9] Cf. my book, *Den kristna gudsbilden*, pp. 225–234.

can provoke evil, and increase the malice of those who are evil. So the evil assails the good, but it is to its own undoing. Evil overreaches itself; its power is broken when it seems to have prevailed.

3. LAW AND THE WRATH OF GOD

'Law' and 'Wrath,' which are included among the tyrants, evidently stand in a closer relation to God's will than the others. It is true that Death and the devil can also be treated by Luther, as they were by the Fathers, as executants of God's judgment on sin; and even from this point of view the victory of Christ implies that Atonement is thereby made between God and the world. It is, as we have seen, unsound to make a distinction between Christ's victory and the Atonement and to claim that His victory effects not atonement, but only salvation. But while it is possible to attempt such a distinction when the victory over death and the devil is under consideration, it is impossible when Law and the Wrath of God are ranged among the enemies overcome by Christ; for both these are immediate expressions of God's holy will. Or, if it is just possible to regard Law, or the Jewish Law, as in a sense separable from God's will, as being a code of ordinances established by Him, it is wholly impossible to regard the Wrath of God as anything else than one aspect of the will of God itself.

Luther often describes in realistic language how the Law assailed Christ but could not enthral Him. He speaks of the Law in the same language as that in which Chrysostom spoke of the devil as attacking Christ, but exceeding his rights and therefore losing them. So the Law, says Luther, condemns Christ, over whom it had no authority, and therefore loses its dominion. "Thou hearest that Christ was caught in the bondage in which we all were held, was set under the Law, was a man full of all grace, righteousness, etc., full of life, yea, He was even the Life itself; now comes the Law and casts itself at Him and would deal with Him as with all other men. Christ sees this, lets the tyrant perform his will upon Him, lets the reproach of all guilt fall against Himself as one accursed, yea, bears the name that He Himself is the curse, and goes to suffer for this cause, dies, and is buried. Now, thinks the Law, He is overpowered; but it knew not that it had so grievously mistaken itself, and that it had condemned and throttled the Son of God; and since it has now judged and condemned Him, who was guiltless and over whom it had no authority, it must in its turn be taken, and see itself made captive and crucified, and lose all its power, and lie under the feet of Him whom it had condemned."[10]

In order to understand the real bearing of such passages in Luther, we must fix the sense in which he regards the Law as an 'enemy.' He maintains, not less vigorously than Paul himself, that the Law is at once good and evil; from one point of view, altogether good; from another, altogether evil. It is good, as an expression of God's will and commandment; yet it is also a 'tyrant,' for it provokes to sin and increases sin. It is not merely that Law stands as a judge of sinful man's failure to keep it, so that it can only lead to condemnation; it is, much more, that the observance of Law is a way that can never lead to salvation. The way of Law is exposed as a false way, a way of works, a Pelagian way, a way by which man seeks to ascend to God. Law, as an expression of God's will, demands that man shall obey freely, voluntarily, not as a mere matter of duty; but at the same time, Law, by the fact that it consists of commandments, sets man in a legal relation to God, characterised by ordinances given in order to be obeyed. "The Law demanded freedom, while at the same time it laid man in bondage. . . . Its demand was therefore impossible to observe from the moment of its

---

[10] Luther's *Works*, XXIII., p. 709; Bring, p. 159.

promulgation. Its function came throughout to be that of the condemning tyrant who judges, and, in so far as he is effective, must condemn."[11] The point is that the very deepening of the demand of Law to include, not merely observance of external commands, but also the spontaneous obedience of love, makes the whole legalistic way impossible, and turns Law into an 'enemy.' This fundamental thought of Luther shows that the idea of Law as regulating the relations of man with God can never set the spiritual life on its right basis, nay, rather destroys it.

Such is the train of thought that lies behind Luther's language about Christ's victory over Law and His deposition of it from its place. The nerve of the whole is the idea of the Divine Love breaking in pieces the order of merit and justice, and creating a new order to govern the relation of man with God, that of Grace. This victory of Christ over Law is the most pointed of all expressions of Luther's opposition to the moralism of Latin Christianity. It needs at the same time to be added, that this basic idea of Law as an enemy is by no means contradicted by what he has to say elsewhere about the value of law and rule for the regulation of the life of the Christian.

The idea of the Wrath of God as an 'enemy' from which Christ delivers us, leads us to the very heart of Luther's theology. Luther used to boast that he had spoken more strongly of the Divine Wrath than had been done under the Pope; and the assertion was not unjustifiable. In the common mediæval teaching, the Wrath of God was relegated to the judgment to come; in Luther, it is set forth as operative in the present, as resting even now, in all its awfulness, on sinful and guilt-laden man. The importance of this point for the discussion of the Atonement is that in Luther the Wrath of God takes the place of the retributive justice (*justitia dis-*

[11] Bring, pp. 166 *f.*

tributiva) of the mediæval scheme. It is typical that Luther
should prefer the personal term to the chilly juridical term;
evidently he is determined to show that God is intensely active and personally engaged in judging sinful man and maintaining the order of Grace which He has established. The
Wrath of God is the expressive phrase that shows God's
will in its immediate and direct reaction to man's sin.

But though the Wrath of God is identical with His will,
yet it is, according to Luther, a 'tyrant,' even the most awful
and terrible of all the tyrants. It is a tyrant in that it stands
opposed to the Divine Love. At this point the idea of God's
own conflict and victory is brought by Luther to a paradoxical sharpness beyond anything that we have hitherto
met; it would seem almost as if the conflict were carried back
within the Divine Being itself. Let us look again at part of
our previous quotation from the *Commentary on Galatians:*
"The curse, which is *the wrath of God* against the whole
world, was in conflict with the blessing—that is to say, with
God's eternal grace and mercy in Christ. The curse conflicts
with the blessing, and would condemn it and altogether annihilate it, but it cannot. For the blessing is *divine and eternal,* therefore the curse must yield. For *if the blessing in
Christ could yield, then God Himself would have been overcome*. But that is impossible."

Luther presents us here with an antinomy, a conflict, between the Divine curse, the Wrath, and the Divine blessing,
the Love. The wrath is the Wrath of God; yet it is the blessing that represents His inmost nature. The curse must give
way; for if the blessing could give way God Himself would
have been defeated. Thus the victory that is won by the Divine "blessing in Christ" is altogether God's own act of victory; for *even at this point* the dualistic outlook is maintained.

It is important to compare this train of thought with that

of the Latin theory of the Atonement. That theory also contains the thought of an opposition between the retributive justice of God on the one hand, and His Love on the other. There is here a real similarity of thought; the chief difference is that in Luther the opposition is presented in a far more acute form. But the two solutions of the antinomy are poles apart. For the Latin theory, the satisfaction made by Christ is primarily a rationally conceived compromise between the demand for punishment and the remission of punishment; the demand of God's justice is satisfied by the compensation paid by Christ from man's side, from below. But in Luther every trace of this rationalism has disappeared; it disappears, because the dualistic outlook is maintained, and because the victory over the Curse and the Wrath is in the fullest sense God's victory. It is God's act of victory, when Christ goes in under the Divine wrath, and bears the burden of the punishment which on account of that wrath impends upon men. Thus the Love of God breaks through the Wrath; in the vicarious act of redemption the Wrath is overcome by the Love which is ultimately, as Luther says, *die Natur Gottes*. But the fact that the Wrath is overcome means not at all that it is to be regarded as only a pretended wrath, or that it ceases to exist; rather, through the Atonement it is *aufgehoben*, transcended, in the Hegelian sense— that is, it remains latent in and behind the Divine Love, and forms the background of the work which the Love fulfils.

Therefore the comparison of this thought of Luther with the corresponding point in the Latin doctrine shows the most radical divergence just where there had been at first sight a similarity. This fact, as we shall see in the next section, has been the occasion of much misunderstanding of Luther's meaning. We find in him a similarity of terminology to some extent with the Latin doctrine, as when he speaks of the vicarious sufferings of Christ, and His endurance of punishment; but these terms bear with him an entirely different meaning, *because* he retains throughout the dualistic outlook and therefore regards God Himself as engaged in the work of redemption. In presenting this theme of the overcoming of the Divine Wrath, he gives the characteristic teaching of the classic idea, but with a greater depth and penetration than ever before. It is the essential double-sidedness of the classic idea—namely, that God is at once the Reconciler and the Reconciled—but it is exhibited in a new and intense light.

4. LUTHER AND THE LATIN DOCTRINE OF THE ATONEMENT

We have already seen the central difference between Luther's teaching on the Atonement and the Latin theory. It is necessary, however, to illustrate the point further by a consideration of Luther's use of certain terms which are specially associated with the Latin theory: in particular, 'sacrifice,' 'merit,' and 'satisfaction.'

The use of these terms by Luther has commonly been taken as proof that his teaching on the Atonement belonged to the Latin type. But the conclusion was far too hastily drawn.

While it is true that the terms Merit and Satisfaction have belonged to the Latin doctrine from its beginnings, this is by no means the case with Sacrifice. We have found the idea of sacrifice used for the expression of the classic idea of the Atonement as early as we can trace it back. And, indeed, Luther's use of this idea agrees closely with that of the early church; there is the same double aspect, of God as at once making the sacrifice and receiving it.

Luther loves to speak of the Sacrifice of Christ as the one true Sacrifice, in contrast with the sacrifices offered by men; and this particularly in his polemic against the sacrifice of the Mass, which was for him the great abomination in the

Latin Mass. This refusal to admit any man-made sacrifice, which could be thought of as an offering made to propitiate God, indicates that the sacrifice of Christ cannot be for him an offering made purely by Christ's human nature, or capable of being interpreted as required by a legal scheme. The sacrifice is God's own sacrifice, while at the same time it can be regarded as offered to God; but Luther's chief interest is to show how much the atoning work (if the phrase may be allowed) *costs* God. His view is also illustrated by the fact that he can introduce side by side with it the thought of the sacrificial self-oblation of Christians; as Christ offered Himself, so must they. If now we remember how definite is Luther's refusal to admit any sacrifice offered by man to God, in order to influence Him as it were from below, this also will help to show that he did not interpret Christ's sacrifice in that sense.

The case is somewhat different with regard to the other two terms, Merit and Satisfaction. They had always belonged to the Latin theory; but Luther throws them into the melting-pot, and gives them a new sense. He uses the term 'Christ's merits' in close connection with the idea of God's grace and mercy towards men. "The merits of Christ are spirit and life, grace and truth."[12] Thus the words of the General Confession in the Swedish Liturgy (which were, however, not inserted in it till 1693) "In Thy fatherly mercy and the merits of the Saviour, Jesus Christ," would have seemed to Luther a mere tautology. Just as he sets the sacrifice of Christ in contrast with all man-made sacrifices, so he contrasts the merits of Christ with all and every merit that men might claim for themselves; for to this point, above all, he was specially alive, that there is no such thing as any human merit or righteousness, but only the goodness of God,

---

[12] "Merita Christi sunt spiritus et vita, sunt gratia et veritas"; Luther's *Works*, II., p. 427; Bring, p. 182, *cf.* pp. 175 ff.

the righteousness of God, manifested in Christ. Thus 'the merits of Christ' mean the same thing as the work of Christ; Justification is altogether the fruit of God's redeeming work; the righteousness of which men can partake depends wholly on God's grace.

With regard to Satisfaction, it is well known that Luther spoke very severely about the use of this word: we will not allow it, he says, in our schools or on the lips of our preachers, but would rather send it back to the judges, advocates, and hangmen, from whom the Pope stole it.[18] If in spite of this Luther could use the word of the work of Christ, the case is parallel to his use of the term Merit. He speaks of satisfaction in relation to the wrath of God, and this association gives us at once his meaning. His conception of the wrath of God and the way in which it is overcome shows that there is no thought here of a satisfaction of the legal claims of the Divine justice; for it is God Himself, the Divine blessing, which in Christ prevails over the wrath and the curse. Thus the term Satisfaction in Luther's mouth exhibits the strength of the Divine Love, which could go in under the punishment that impended upon men. The satisfaction is made *by* God, not merely *to* God.

The essential point is that Luther uses both these terms, Merit and Satisfaction, in direct relation to Christ's conflict and His victory over the 'tyrants'; even these words he incorporates into the dualistic scheme. There is not the least reason to suppose that when he does this there are two trains of thought running side by side in his mind, least of all two inconsistent trains of thought. Every attempt to prove that Luther's teaching contains an idea of 'satisfaction' other than that involved in the triumph of Christ over the tyrants is doomed to hopeless failure. Least of all is it possible to dis-

-³ *Luther's Works*, XXXIV., i., pp. 301 *f.*; Bring, p. 176.

tinguish in him an idea of an atoning work as different from the work of redemption or salvation. To attempt this is to seek to measure Luther by the standards of the Latin theory. He knows no such distinction; for him salvation is atonement and atonement salvation.

Nothing, therefore, can be more incorrect than to speak of Luther's occasional use of the term Satisfaction as if the passages in which this term occurs gave us his doctrine of the Atonement properly so called. I will give one very characteristic example of the way in which he passes from the mention of the satisfaction to that of Christ's conflict and victory. Faith, he writes, depends on this, and consists in this, "that we firmly believe that Christ, the Son of God, stood for us and took all our sins upon His neck, and is the eternal satisfaction for our sins, and made atonement for us to God the Father; he that believes this has a place also in this sacrament (Holy Communion), and neither the devil, hell, nor sin can harm him. Wherefore? Because God is his defence and his helper, and if I thus have believed, therefore I know surely that God fights for me, in spite of the devil, death, hell, and sin, which would harm me; this is the great inestimable treasure which is given to us in Christ." [14]

But there is one more point that must not be omitted in this connection. The traditional text of Luther is not always to be trusted. In certain passages where Luther speaks of the merits of Christ and His satisfaction, Bring has proved that the text has been amended in order to bring it into line with the Latin doctrine. Thus, the traditional text of the *Commentary on Galatians*, on ch. v. 1, reads thus: "The liberty with which Christ has made us free is not from some sort of bondage to men, or the power of the tyrants, but from the everlasting wrath of God." But the Rörer MS. reads: "It is a

[14] Luther's *Works*, X., iii., p. 49; Bring, p. 186.

liberty from the Law, from sins, death, the power of the devil, the wrath of God, the last judgment."[15] Therefore the true text shows that, so far from contrasting the power of the tyrants with the wrath of God, in this passage as in others he ranges the wrath of God as one of the tyrants from which Christ delivers us. Such disorders in the text are not to be treated as accidental. They shed an interesting light on the extent to which Luther's contemporaries failed to understand him.

We have said enough to show that the common interpretation of Luther's teaching on the Atonement along the lines of the Latin theory is altogether on wrong lines. It has, indeed, only been possible because arguments were based on terms and not on the meanings actually given to them, because his teaching on the Atonement was taken in isolation from the rest of his theology, and because there has been little perception of the meaning of the classic idea of the Atonement. The only alternative to the Latin doctrine of the Atonement that was known to exist was the so-called subjective view; and the evident fact that Luther's teaching on the Atonement was fully 'objective,' and contained the idea of vicarious suffering, seemed sufficient proof that it was to be ranged with that of Anselm.

But nothing can be more misleading. Luther's teaching on the Atonement cannot be isolated from the rest of his teaching; and from first to last it involves the view of Christ's work as a conflict and a triumph. The structure of his thought is such that the Latin doctrine of the Atonement simply cannot be fitted into it. The presupposition of the Latin theory was the moralistic idea of penance; but that

[15] The original Latin is as follows: Traditional text: "ea (libertas) est, qua Christus nos liberavit, non e servitute aliqua humana aut vi Tyrannorum, sed ira Dei æterna."

The Rörer MS.: "est libertas a lege, peccatis, morte, a potentia diaboli, ira Dei, extremo iudicio" (Bring, pp. 180–182).

was for Luther an abomination. The Latin doctrine involved the idea of law and justice as the typical expression of God's relation to man; but this is just what Luther tears in pieces, raising God's claim to a higher level, and therefore treating Law as, in one aspect, a tyrant from which man needs to be delivered. The structure of the Latin theory is rational throughout; Luther, if he is sure of anything, is sure that God's work in Christ of atonement, forgiveness, justification, bears the signature *contra rationem et legem*. In his view, Law and Reason belong inseparably together; they represent the way of the natural man, not God's way manifested in Christ. Thus the implication of the Latin theory, that the work of God in the Atonement is interrupted by an offering made to God from man's side, is radically opposed to that which is the very centre of Luther's thought—namely, that there is no way by which man may go to God other than the way which God Himself has made in becoming man.

Finally, as we saw, the difference between Luther's teaching and that of the Latin theory becomes clearest of all at the very point where for a moment they seemed to run parallel. Luther's language about the Divine Love and the Divine Wrath may truly be said to correspond to that of the Latin doctrine about the Divine Love and the Divine Justice. But just at this point Luther turns the train of thought the other way up, refusing to contemplate a rational solution of the difficulty, but rather insisting on the triumph of the Divine Love over the Divine Wrath by the way of self-oblation for our sake.

Therefore Luther stands out in the history of Christian doctrine as the man who expressed the classic idea of the Atonement with greater power than any before him. From the side-line of the Latin theory he bends right back to the main line, making a direct connection with the teaching of the New Testament and the Fathers. This is his claim to be regarded as in the true sense of the word, catholic. But he is a solitary figure. The doctrine of Lutheranism became a very different thing from that of Luther.

7

SINCE THE REFORMATION

I. LUTHER AND HIS SUCCESSORS

LUTHER'S teaching on the Atonement was not followed either by his contemporaries or by his successors. Perhaps there is no single point at which the men of that age showed such complete incapacity to grasp his meaning. Without hesitation and without delay they reverted to the Latin doctrine; for the tradition was fixed long before the period of Lutheran Orthodoxy.

The fact is on the face of it extraordinarily baffling. The classic idea of the Atonement had been set forth by Luther with unique power, and expressed with supreme clearness. It was not hidden away in his less accessible writings such as the *De servo arbitrio;* it pervaded all his work, but especially his most popular pieces, his Catechisms and his hymns. Further, this idea of the Atonement formed one organic whole with the central proclamation of the Reformation; and Luther's authority was immense. It might then have been anticipated that the perpetuation of the classic teaching on the Atonement was assured; yet it is evident that the opposite was the case.

Obviously, Luther's contemporaries failed to understand his teaching on this subject, and they never grasped his deeper thoughts. They interpreted him from the first in the light of the traditional belief inherited from the Middle Ages. Either they failed to see the gulf which separated him from the scholastic theologians, or, in so far as they had some inkling of it, they did their best to cover it up. We have noted the clear evidence of tampering with the text of his writings.

The man who stood nearest to Luther himself in the Reformation movement was a man predisposed by his whole mental outlook to guide its theology on other lines. There is no doubt that Melanchthon rendered immense services to the Lutheran Reformation; but, that in restating Luther's theology he blunted its edge and rationalised it, has been revealed in ever clearer light by the new and deeper study of Luther which has been carried out, chiefly in Sweden and in Germany, in the last thirty years. Melanchthon's reintroduction of the Aristotelian philosophy brought his thought at once into line with mediæval scholasticism; and, indeed, it was always his chief interest to achieve rational and lucid theological explanations. The inner tensions within Luther's theology, the vigour and force of his thoughts, and his sharply paradoxical language, Melanchthon wholly lacked the power to understand. Even from the point of view of formal theology, he was a man of compromise; this is seen everywhere, in his attitude to the *De servo arbitrio*, in his restatement of the doctrine of Justification, but most clearly of all in his treatment of the Atonement. The issue was brought to a point in the controversy with Osiander, which had a decisive influence on the subsequent development of the Lutheran doctrine; we shall therefore shortly return to it. But as early as 1542, in the *Loci præcipui theologici*, Melanchthon had given a statement of the doctrine of the Atonement fundamentally in accord with the scholastic scheme. The Latin type had returned.

How is this change of front to be explained? We have already noted that part of the explanation may be the employment by Luther of the terminology proper to the Latin doctrine. He had, indeed, given the terms in question a new meaning and placed them in a new context; but the fact that he had used them involved at once the risk that others would take from him the terms, and miss their new connections and their new significance. The terms had had a long history, and carried old associations from which it was not easy to shake them free. It must also be remembered that the doctrine of the Atonement was not commonly reckoned as one of the controversial issues; Luther's teaching on this subject had not been directly polemical, like his teaching on Justification, and (partly) his teaching on the church, and had therefore attracted less attention. It is worth while remarking that theological controversy is not always an unmixed evil. Time and again a pointed formula to which some controversy has given birth has served as a protective covering, to save some positive insight into truth from being lost and forgotten.

Above all, it is necessary to see that in the history of Christian thought Luther stands as a veritable colossus. We might refer, for the sake of a comparison, to the appreciation of Kant by his contemporaries and successors. It is a commonplace that Kant's most central philosophical criticisms were seriously distorted by those who believed themselves to be continuing his work; for the philosophical revolution involved in Kant's teaching was too thorough-going to be fully understood and accepted at once. If, however, this comparison between Kant and Luther is to be made to yield its full value, two qualifications must be borne in mind: First, that while Kant took the greatest pains to express himself with all possible accuracy, Luther was in this respect quite careless and reckless; and, second, that the revolution for which Luther stood in the sphere of Christian teaching was not less but more thorough than that of Kant in the sphere of philosophy. These considerations will help to show that it is not so surprising, after all, that Luther's teaching was so largely misunderstood by his would-be followers.

We may now pass on to consider the controversy with Osiander, which marks the chief turning-point on the road from Luther to Lutheran Orthodoxy. This controversy was concerned primarily with Justification, but it spread over the whole central field of Christian doctrine. Its result was to establish the authority of a view of God's righteousness and of law, which firmly fixed the accepted doctrine of the Atonement in the line of the Latin tradition.

The tragedy of the debate on Justification between Osiander on the one side, and Melanchthon, Mörlin, and others on the other, was that both sides could claim to appeal to Luther, but that neither side had grasped anything like his whole width of view. It may be truly said that Melanchthon faithfully upheld the central idea of the Reformation, God's gracious acceptance of sinful man; but he did not preserve the idea intact, and only at the price of its incorporation into a rigid legalistic scheme and of the loss of much of its original richness. The result was the strange association of an anti-moralistic doctrine of *sola gratia* and a legalistic view of man's relation to God, which came as a result to be typical of Protestant Orthodoxy.

Mörlin, in opposition to Osiander, emphasised the view of God's righteousness as exclusively retributive and punitive justice, which became thenceforth the accepted doctrine; thus Luther's teaching on the meaning of God's righteousness passed out of sight. E. Hirsch puts the matter thus: that God's righteousness, treated as equivalent to retributive justice, becomes the governing idea of the conception of God, and at this central point the Gospel is obscured by 'nomism.' "The pre-Lutheran idea of the Divine righteousness, *admitted by preference into the Anselmian-Melanchthonian scheme,* perverted the original Protestant conception of God."[1]

The result was that Law now came to be taken as the essential basis of man's relation to God; to use again Brunner's phrase, it was accepted as the granite-foundation of the spiritual world. Luther's fundamental thought, that Law is in one aspect a tyrant and an enemy from whose power Christ came to set men free, is altogether lost. Law provides now the scheme by which it is necessary to interpret everything, even God's salvation through Christ. Mörlin is clear enough: "Perfect obedience to God's Law, perfect fulfilment of that Law, is necessary to salvation."[2] God is primarily regarded as the Judge who punishes transgression. This gives the context in which the work of Christ is interpreted: He has offered to God in our stead the obedience required by retributive justice. Our share in eternal life is regarded as a reward for the righteousness of Christ imputed to us.

Flacius speaks in a similar strain. He describes the imputation to us of Christ's obedience as a transference made by God at the request of both parties, Christ and men. Consequently he prefers to speak of the forgiveness of sins as granted, not *gratis*, but *precario;* the former term would only be partly true, but the latter he regards as strictly accurate.

A further illustration of this narrowing of outlook, or rather complete change of front, is given by the emphasis now laid on the 'natural knowledge of God.' To justify his view of the Divine righteousness, Mörlin argues that *even according to natural theology* retributive justice stands out as the primary attribute of God. Such a proposition reveals

[1] *Die Theologie des Andreas Osiander,* p. 246.
[2] "Obœdientia legis perfecta seu impletio legis est ad salutem necessaria."

as in a flash the essential opposition of this doctrine to that of Luther; and Mörlin is able to appeal here to the authority of Melanchthon. For Melanchthon, in his explanation of *lumen naturæ*, maintains that the Law of God is, on the one side, the truth granted to human reason; on the other, the supreme norm of the Divine Will. Retributive justice thus becomes the essential element in this view of Law. It is not unjust to say with Hirsch that Melanchthon is the real father of the 'rational nomism' of Protestant Orthodoxy.

2. THE DOCTRINE OF THE ATONEMENT IN PROTESTANT ORTHODOXY

The typical Latin outlook on the Atonement thus regained control of Protestant theology long before it found definite expression in a theory of the Atonement. I shall now give a sketch of the leading characteristics of the teaching of Protestant Orthodoxy on this subject, and seek to fix its place in the history of Christian doctrine. This can readily be done, because this teaching is remarkably uniform, far more uniform than the mediæval doctrine in the period subsequent to Anselm.

The doctrine of the Atonement in Lutheran Orthodoxy is not simply identical with that of Anselm; but the differences must not be exaggerated, and they do not in the least involve any departure from the essential Latin type. The strange thing is that the mediæval doctrine of the Atonement remained, in a slightly modified form, while the penitential system and the idea of penance, on which it had originally been built up, had completely disappeared.

The broad similarity of this doctrine with that of Anselm consists primarily in the fact that the whole conception is dominated by the idea of Satisfaction; the satisfaction is treated as a rational necessity, the only possible method by which Atonement can be effected. Protestant Orthodoxy thus follows Anselm more closely than the usual mediæval teaching. It states the problem in the same way; it repeats the contention that the payment of the satisfaction is the only alternative to a condonation of laxity. One or the other there must be; either a love which in forgiving violates the demands of justice, or else satisfaction. No other alternative is regarded as conceivable.

The divergence of the Protestant doctrine from that of Anselm is often held to consist largely in this: that it treats the satisfaction made by Christ as being also an endurance of punishment; the sin of man had deserved punishment, punishment is the inexorable demand of justice, and, therefore, Christ endures it instead of men. But, as we saw in an earlier chapter, this idea belongs naturally to the Latin doctrine, and it occurs quite frequently in the later Middle Ages; indeed, it can be found even in Anselm himself. It is a far more important difference that in the Protestant doctrine the satisfaction is regarded as made not merely by the death of Christ, but by His whole fulfilment of God's law throughout His life—that is, by His *obœdientia activa*. This may be truly called a development of the earlier doctrine; an important addition has been made to it. The life of Christ as a whole is now held to avail for the satisfaction of God's justice. Yet even this development does not involve any abandonment of the essential Latin idea; it might rather be said that the Latin idea is now more fully worked through to its logical conclusion than ever before.

It is the legal structure of the Latin doctrine that is now more dominant than even Anselm had ever made it. It is now not merely that the retributive justice of God must be satisfied by Christ's death, but that Law, as representing God's *justitia legislativa*, must be satisfied also; there can be no atonement unless man has fulfilled all God's commandments. Hence there is a double necessity: Christ must by His *obœdientia activa* fulfil God's law to the uttermost, and He must by His death pay the penalty which justice requires for man's transgression of it.

If, then, it is true of the Latin doctrine of the Atonement in general that it is wholly comprehended within a rigid legal scheme, it is doubly true of the Protestant form of that doctrine. The thoroughness of the logical consistency with which the legal idea is carried through gives it a monumental character; the impression which it gives is that of a massive building in a solid and austere style, capable of withstanding the storms of centuries.

The idea of God which underlies it is, above all, that of a Justice which imposes its law and demands satisfaction; only within these limits is the Divine Love allowed to operate, and there is a suggestion that the idea of the Divine Love is regarded with some suspicion, as though it needed to be watched lest it should infringe on the demands of justice. The *motif* of the whole idea is Law; and it is significant that it is from the Old Testament that this theology always prefers to draw its 'scriptural proofs' of the rational necessity of satisfaction, and that a number of New Testament texts cause evident difficulty. The satisfaction given through the vicarious obedience and the vicarious punishment of Christ is the logical compromise between condemnation and free forgiveness, the guarantee that Love does not become laxity; the word 'compensation,' typical of the Protestant form of the Latin doctrine, expresses exactly that which the justice of God must demand, in order that His Mercy may be free to act. So the opposition of the Divine Justice and Mercy is reconciled, and He is able to forgive.

It is true, of course, that the act of God in justifying man is treated as an act of His Mercy as much as of His Justice. God's *gratia* is shown in His readiness to accept the satisfaction offered by Another, and impute it to sinful men. To this

extent the legal idea is not pushed to its extreme limit—
though we may note in passing that even this was done by
the nineteenth-century theologian Philippi, who taught that,
since God had through Christ's satisfaction received adequate compensation for our fault, "we could even demand
everlasting life from God's justice."[3] Yet even the act of
God's mercy in forgiving does not transgress the limits of
law and justice. Nothing was less to the taste of the Orthodoxy of the eighteenth century than Luther's *contra legem;*
and the whole theological structure was intended to show
that there was nothing irrational, nothing contrary to strict
justice, in the forgiveness bestowed by God. Anselm's *nihil
rationabilius* still remains typical of the whole doctrine.

At the same time it is clear that God's work in the Atonement is to be represented, not by a continuous line, as in the
New Testament, the Fathers, and Luther, but, as in Anselm,
by a broken line; for the compensation is paid by Christ as
man, from man's side, in man's stead. It would, indeed, be
unfair to say that God is regularly represented as simply the
recipient of the atoning work, or that His attitude is changed
thereby; for the Atonement is regarded, as it had been by
Anselm, as having its origin in God's will, springing, as was
so often said, out of the Divine mercy as well as of the Divine justice. Nevertheless, it remains true that the Divine operation in the Atonement was regarded as interrupted by the
compensation paid from the human side, from below.

The Lutheran theologians did indeed hold that the satisfaction was made by 'both natures' of Christ, and pointed to
this as a difference between their doctrine and that of 'the
papists.' But in reality this was little more than a verbal difference, a theological refinement: the doctrine of the *com-
municatio idiomatum,* which was elaborated in opposition
to the Calvinists, demanded that both natures should co-

[3] F. A. Philippi, *Christliche Glaubenslehre,* IV., 2, p. 38.

operate in the work of atonement. But in reality the difference from the mediæval doctrine was only verbal; for the
Divine nature of Christ, which co-operated with the human
nature in virtue of the hypostatic union, was regarded as giving an infinite value to the work effected by the human nature as the 'agent.' Thus in effect the old answer to the question was still given, and there still remained the same lack of
organic connection between the Incarnation and the Atonement which had always been typical of the Latin doctrine.

Thus the doctrine of the Atonement in Protestant Orthodoxy belongs indisputably to the Latin type, and it forms
the clearest and most logical of all the expressions of that
type. During this period the classic idea of the Atonement is
completely suppressed in the realm of theology; for, though
the phrases and images which belong properly to it still occur occasionally, they are mere reminiscences, and play no
part at all in the theological result. It scarcely needs to be
said that the preaching of the period usually reflected the accepted doctrine, since the preachers were much more dominated by the ruling theology and less influenced by the liturgy than had been the case in the Middle Ages. The case is,
however, somewhat different in regard to the hymns. The
Passion hymns naturally bear the marks of the dominant theology; at the same time we find in them, from an early date,
the influence of the same devotion to the Passion of Christ
which had been typical of the Middle Ages. This is not surprising, since the devotional literature of the Reformation
was largely based on the mediæval tradition. We return thus
to the interesting analogy which we have already noted, between the late mediæval period and that of Protestant
Orthodoxy; in both cases a rationalised theology provokes
by way of reaction an emotional piety, which is partly com-
plementary to it, and partly a contrast to it. This devotion to
the Passion was strongly taken up by the Pietists.

On the other hand, the Easter hymns continued to reflect the classic idea; so, for instance, in the seventeenth-century hymn-books of the Swedish Church the Easter hymns still sound the note of the Divine conflict and triumph. The Paschal season has never ceased to be the impregnable citadel of the classic idea of the Atonement.

3. THE ARRIVAL OF THE 'SUBJECTIVE' OR HUMANISTIC DOCTRINE

The doctrine of the Atonement came to be regarded as the palladium of Orthodox Protestantism; only the doctrine of the verbal inspiration of the Bible can be compared with it in importance from this point of view. It ranked then as the typical and representative embodiment of the genius of this Orthodoxy; it was regarded as 'the church doctrine' of the Atonement *par excellence,* as if it and it alone had been the teaching of orthodox Christians through all the centuries.

Therefore the assault of the Enlightenment on the Orthodox theology concentrated itself on the doctrine of the Atonement. It was subjected to a fierce theological criticism, partly similar to that of the Nominalists three centuries before; the difference was that the theologians of the Enlightenment had no respect for the church authority which the doctrine enjoyed. In the course of the eighteenth century, the doctrine became in a measure disintegrated by the assaults made upon it; but in the nineteenth century it enjoyed something of a revival, and, though it failed to regain the leadership of the theological world, it recovered sufficient strength to maintain the controversy, and to give rise to a number of mediating theories.

The decline of the doctrine really begins with Pietism, for, though it is only the more radical forms of Pietism that show any conscious opposition to it, it is here that the first definite signs appear of a movement in the subjectivist direction. The Pietistic writers often show a preference for imagery, such as Christ the Physician of the soul, over the legal language of the Orthodox doctrine; sometimes, as in Spener, we meet again the old imagery of the classic type. This last feature is probably to be explained by the deliberate use by the Pietists of the New Testament rather than the Old; and this was bound to undermine the supremacy of a legalistic doctrine of the Atonement. But the most important point of all, in view of the future, was that the watchword of Pietism was New Birth (*Wiedergeburt*) rather than Justification—that is to say, the word chosen was one that described a subjective process.

But for the theologians of the Enlightenment, the controversy against the 'Orthodox' doctrine of the Atonement became a matter of primary concern. The criticism of the Latin theory had begun with Abelard, and had never been completely silenced; now it dominated the situation. All the bases of the Orthodox theory were challenged. A 'more human' idea of the Atonement was propounded, to replace the accepted 'juridical' treatment. The idea of sin was made relative; sin was regarded as a state of imperfection. The doctrine of retributive punishment was scouted, for punishment could only be ameliorative. Above all, these theologians desired to uproot the 'anthropomorphic' features and 'relics of Judaism' from the conception of God; the idea of God that lay behind the Orthodox doctrine of the Atonement was inconsistent with the 'simple teaching' of Jesus, and the love of the Heavenly Father. It was therefore intolerable that God should be thought of as needing to be 'propitiated' through a satisfaction offered to Him. The death of Jesus could not rightly be interpreted in this way—so far all agreed; it was understood in various ways, as a seal set upon His teaching, as a vindication of the moral order of the universe, as a lofty example, as a symbolical expression of God's readiness to be reconciled. Only in some such sense could the work of Christ rightly be connected with the Atonement.

It was an axiom of the enlightenment that God's attitude to the world must, always and unalterably, be one of benevolence and goodwill; such language was preferred to the word Love. Therefore, so far as God was concerned, no Atonement was needed. It is therefore a little surprising that, side by side with this emphasis on God's unchanging goodwill, the idea appears of a certain influence exerted upon God from man's side. Man repents and amends his life, and God in turn responds by rewarding man's amendment with an increase of happiness. The ruling idea is therefore essentially anthropocentric and moralistic.

In result, it might appear that the Orthodox theologians had been right after all. They had always said that the only alternative to the Satisfaction of God's justice was a love which spelt laxity; and now it was clear that the rejection of the Orthodox doctrine of satisfaction actually involved a weakening of the idea of sin, and a toning-down of the radical opposition of the will of God to that which is evil. If, then, we, for our part, have refused to accept the Orthodox dilemma as valid, we can only do so because we have learnt to distinguish another idea of the Atonement, which both Orthodox Protestantism and the Enlightenment had left out of count: the classic idea.

4. THE NINETEENTH CENTURY

The nineteenth century is characterised by a continuous conflict between the 'subjective' and the 'objective' views of the Atonement. The latter had survived the assaults of the Enlightenment, and had succeeded in gathering its forces to make a more vigorous resistance; but the hegemony lay with the other side. It is true that, from Schleiermacher onwards, the theology of the Enlightenment was not simply reproduced; it was criticised as shallow, and an endeavour was made to deepen it. Yet these theologians show a closer continuity with the Enlightenment than they themselves believed; this is true not least of Schleiermacher himself. There was the same humanistic and anthropomorphic outlook in their teaching on the Atonement as in their theology in general.

The feature which first arrests our attention in Schleiermacher is his distinction between *Erlösung* and *Versöhnung*, Salvation and Atonement. Salvation takes the primary place; it is effected as the individual's sense of God grows stronger. Atonement, reconciliation, is the sense of blessedness, which follows on a deepened consciousness of God. This distinction was of special importance in nineteenth-century theology, and it well illustrates the anthropocentric outlook. Schleiermacher says quite plainly that the change in the spiritual life which comes to pass as the soul's consciousness of God is deepened, is the real meaning of that which is called atonement.

It is particularly interesting to note the order in which the two ideas, Salvation and Atonement, are arranged. Wherever the classic idea of the Atonement is dominant, the two coincide; alike in the early church and in Luther, Salvation is Atonement, and Atonement is Salvation. With the Latin doctrine the case is different; Atonement is treated as prior to Salvation, a preliminary to it, making the subsequent process of salvation possible. But Schleiermacher reverses the order; Salvation (the change in the spiritual life) comes first, and Atonement (Reconciliation) follows as its completion.

It would be possible to object that this comparison is misleading, because the terms in question are being used in different senses. Even so, it has its value. It shows that the change in the meaning of the terms follows directly upon the change of order. Schleiermacher, with his anthropocentric outlook, interprets salvation primarily as a *Lebenserhöhung*, or moral uplift; Atonement, or Reconciliation, becomes essentially a sense of being at home in the cosmos, gained through the uplift of the soul, or a new attitude to life, characterised by harmony with the universe. Man comes to understand that all things are dependent on God, and, therefore, that which seems to disturb the harmony of things does so only in appearance. It might be said that 'Atonement' in this sense means that man is reconciled with his situation and his environment. The subjectivity of the whole conception is in any case evident.

The place of Christ and Christ's work in this scheme is consistent with the rest. The anthropocentric attitude is not modified when He comes into consideration. Christ is regarded as the starting-point of the influences that work towards the strengthening of man's consciousness of God, because He is the embodiment of the ideal of religion, the Pattern Man, who has an absolutely perfect and blessed consciousness of God. But it is not necessary for our purpose to go more fully into Schleiermacher's dialectically interesting discussion of the Latin doctrine of the Atonement and of earlier forms of teaching. God is not regarded as having any direct relation to the process of man's reconciliation, except in so far as He is the ultimate sanction of man's sense of 'absolute dependence.' When all is governed by universal causality, there is no room for an Atonement in the sense of the removal of an alienation between God and man. No such alienation can be believed to exist, since the active hostility of the Divine Love towards evil has faded away and the dualistic outlook has been banished by the monism which dominates the view. In so far as this is used to explain God's relation to Christ and His work, the prevailing idea is that Christ is treated as the Head of the human race, and that

God's attitude to mankind is influenced by the fact that He sees mankind in the light which radiates from Christ.

Ritschl, in his great work *Rechtfertigung und Versöhnung*, maintains essentially the same line of thought. Like all the writers of this school, he gives us a vigorous criticism of the 'juridical' doctrine of the Atonement; but he is blind to the significance of the classic idea, and summarily dismisses its imagery whenever it comes under discussion. The title of his book shows an anxiety to do better justice to the Reformation than Schleiermacher had done; 'Justification' in his title takes the place of Schleiermacher's 'Salvation.' Nevertheless, the line of thought is closely parallel. The central point for Ritschl is that man gives up his mistrust of God, which had been based on a misunderstanding of God's character, and is dissipated by the sight of Christ's faithfulness to His vocation even unto death; this human faithfulness is a revelation of the Divine Love. As with Schleiermacher, Atonement follows subsequently, as the result of man's new relation to God, and signifies primarily a new relation to the world, characterised by *Selbstbehauptung*, self-realisation, and mastery of the world. Here, too, the anthropocentric nature of the idea is plain.

The latest work of importance belonging to this general type is *The Idea of Atonement in Christian Theology*, by the late Dr. Rashdall. He, too, works with the distinction of 'objective' and 'subjective' views of the Atonement. By the former he means a theory following the lines of the Latin doctrine; the 'subjective' view he traces back particularly to Abelard, who in this exposition of the subject receives quite a disproportionate share of attention. It is a surprise to find Abelard's theory described as "entirely in harmony with the earlier tradition of the church" (p. 443). Abelard's thought is summed up as follows: "He sees that God can only be supposed to forgive by making the sinner better, and thereby removing any demand for punishment" (p. 359).

No doubt Rashdall may be regarded as comparing favourably with Continental theologians of a similar tendency, in so far as he follows the praiseworthy English tradition in giving a greater place to the Incarnation than the German writers whom we have discussed. Nevertheless, it cannot be said that he gives adequate expression to the Christian idea of the Incarnation; like other idealistic writers, he allows the highest human to shade off into the Divine, and thus obscures the distinction between the Divine and the human. Christ reveals God, because He exhibits the ideal manhood (*cf.* pp. 447 *ff.*). But it is particularly important to see that the question of Salvation is treated by him just as much from the ethical point of view as by Schleiermacher. The following are typical phrases: "The death of Christ justifies us, inasmuch as through it charity is stirred up in our hearts" (p. 438); "the efficacy of Christ's death is attributed to the moral effects which it produces" (p. 443); Christ has taught us "to think of God as a Father who will forgive men their sins if and in proportion as they have repented of them" (p. 461); and "in the two parables of the prodigal son and the Pharisee and the publican, we have the fullest expression of this fundamental idea—that God forgives the truly penitent freely and without any other condition than that of true penitence" (p. 26).

The weakness of this exposition is not to be found in the language about the ethical effects of the Divine forgiveness on human lives; on the contrary, this is its strength. Its weakness is that the forgiving and atoning work of God is *made dependent upon* the ethical effects in human lives; consequently, the Divine Love is not clearly set forth as a free, spontaneous love. Wherever there is such a view of the Divine Love, as not called forth by the worthiness or goodness of men, but as bestowing value on men by the very fact that they are loved by God, the work of the Divine forgiveness always appears as prior to ethical regeneration, not dependent upon or proportioned to human repentance or any other conditions on man's side. It is this primacy of the Divine Love which is the basis of the classic idea of the Atonement as God's own work.

I will now give just one instance of an attempt to mediate by way of compromise between the Latin and the humanistic types of view, which were for the most part in violent opposition to one another during the nineteenth century. It is taken from an essay by the Swedish Archbishop Ekman, which in its day (1906) attracted much attention. It shows how deeply the anthropocentric habit of thought had sunk in, even among those who were anxious not to lose touch with the Latin theory of the Atonement, which was regarded as the church teaching. The Archbishop's leading idea is that "it is simply the conversion of men that effects the Atonement"; hence "God gives up His displeasure against a man, and reverses His sentence of judgment, when the man confesses his sin and asks for pardon, recognises that he has rightly deserved to suffer for his sin, and earnestly applies himself to do God's will." This line of thought is followed out thus: the conversion of the human race is the atonement of mankind; and such a conversion has taken place representatively in Jesus Christ. He is "the true man," He "stands forth as the Head of mankind, and to plead man's cause." This influences God's attitude: "Let us imagine a nation which is universally despised, but among it is a noble hero, who exercises a mighty influence on the nation; then we become reconciled in our thought towards this nation. There radiates from the hero a reconciling light over the nation. . . . So, in the midst of mankind God sees Jesus Christ. He sees a human radiance which scatters its beams over the human race. He sees streaks of truth, purity, and righteousness spreading among men. He sees in the body of mankind a new heart, whose strong pulse is spreading new life through the veins of the body. . . . He has then no further displeasure with mankind seen as a whole, He no longer despairs of mankind, He reconciles Himself with mankind."

The significant thing is that this last passage, which is intended to conserve what is essential in the 'objective' doctrine of the Atonement, contains not the faintest idea of an Atonement effected by God Himself. The approach of man to God is altogether an approach 'from below'; Christ as 'the true man' may be conceived to exercise influence on God's thought of mankind and His relation to mankind; God sees 'a human radiance' illuminating the human race, and therefore reconciles Himself with mankind.

If our sketch of the third of the three main types of Atonement-doctrine has left a less clear impression on the reader's mind than the other two, this is not altogether due to the brevity of our description of it; there is a lack of definite outline in the type itself. This lack of definiteness is reflected in the name which it commonly bears—the 'subjective' doctrine. It would, of course, be absurd so to press this word as to imply that this teaching leaves God wholly out of account and so makes the idea of a true atonement meaningless; but it is true that in this view the emphasis is shifted from that which may be held to be done for men by God or by Christ to that which is done in men and by men.

In order to understand this third type of view, it is important to see that its character is determined by its opposition to the Latin theory. It criticises especially the notion that God needs in any sense to be reconciled or that His attitude to mankind should be changed; any such assertion is inconsistent with His Love. Hence the Love of God is maintained, with a denial of any sort of tension or opposition be-

tween God's mercy and His justice. The question then becomes, whether the Divine Love is so set forth as to conserve the deepest elements of the Christian faith, or whether
there is loss of something essential through over-simplifica-
tion. We shall return to this question in the next chapter.
Here, however, I will add just one point. The 'subjective'
view is anxious to show how there cannot be any influence
exerted upon God so as to propitiate Him or change His
attitude towards man. Yet at the same time this view as-
sumes, even to a greater extent than the Latin view, just such
an influence upon God from man's side. For the extent to
which 'atonement' is effected depends upon that which is
done in and by men, on their penitence, their conversion;
therefore God's attitude to men is really made to depend on
men's attitude to God. The case is not different when Christ
and His work come under consideration. The effect of
Christ's work is that God, seeing the character of Christ,
and His place as the Representative Man, gains a new and
more hopeful view of humanity.

8

THE THREE TYPES

THE HISTORY of the doctrine of the Atonement is a history of three types of view, which emerge in turn. The classic idea emerges with Christianity itself, and remains the dominant type of teaching for a thousand years. The origin of the Latin doctrine can be exactly determined; it belongs to the West, and it becomes the dominant form of the doctrine of the Atonement in the West in the Middle Ages. Though Luther returns to the classic type, and teaches it with unique power, post-Reformation theology goes back to the Latin type, which is therefore common to the scholasticism of both the Roman and the Protestant churches.

We have, then, found some interesting connections, which traverse the commonly accepted scheme. First, we have seen the close connection between the teaching of the Apostolic Age and that of the early church; at the same time a gulf has opened between both these and the scholastic doctrine of the Middle Ages. Then we have seen that Luther's true connections are not only with the New Testament, but also with the Fathers, whose doctrine of the Atonement he reproduces; Luther, therefore, belongs to the Catholic tradition, in the true sense of the word. Then, again, we have seen the connection between the two scholastic periods, that of the

Middle Ages and that of Protestant Orthodoxy; but the closeness of this connection must not be exaggerated, for the fact that Protestantism was seeking to unite the *sola gratia* principle of the Reformation with a juridical doctrine of the Atonement involved it in a fundamental inconsistency.

Between the classic type and the Latin there has been relatively little *direct* controversy. At more than one period it has happened that the upholders of the Latin doctrine have had very little sense of the real opposition between the two types of view; failing altogether to see the real bearings of the classic idea, they have treated it as a hesitating attempt to express that which is adequately set forth in the Latin doctrine.

On the other hand, the controversy between the Latin and the subjective types has been open and avowed from the beginning. The first full statement of the Latin theory by Anselm was followed immediately by the criticisms of Abelard; and the controversy was renewed in full force by the theologians of the Enlightenment. Since that time the controversy has continued with varying fortunes, and it has finally resolved itself into a war of attrition between the two rival doctrines, with no prospect of victory for either side.

Meanwhile the classic idea dropped almost out of sight in the sphere of theology; it has been the common assumption that the other two types of doctrine were the only possible forms which the Christian doctrine of the Atonement can take. Nevertheless, the classic idea has never wholly died out; it was too deeply rooted in the classical formulæ of Christianity to be completely lost. It reappears from time to time in the hymnody of a Wesley in England or a Grundtvig in Denmark. Even in theology, essays in the direction of the classic idea have occasionally been made, by way of softening the rigour of the Latin doctrine, or of giving greater depth to the subjective teaching.

But in these last few years the situation has been changing rapidly. In the course of the long controversy the two rival doctrines have thoroughly exposed one another's weak points; and now it is becoming clearer with every year that passes that they both belong to the past. It is the outstanding characteristic of the theological situation to-day that in many ways and on many sides the humanistic outlook which has been dominant for nearly two hundred years is being fundamentally challenged. Something else is coming to take its place. It is just conceivable that we may see a return to the scholasticism of the preceding period; a tendency in this direction is seen in the so-called Dialectical Theology, in the *Dogmatik* of Karl Barth, which represents a direct contradiction of the Liberal Protestant attitude, and to a lesser extent in E. Brunner.[1] But, at least in regard to the doctrine of the Atonement, a door appears to stand open now, which has been closed for centuries, for the classic idea to come again to the fore; and it would not be hard to find indications in contemporary theological literature that it is already exercising its forces for a great advance.

2. AN ANALYSIS OF THE THREE TYPES

(i.) *Structure.*—We shall now endeavour to sketch out a comparison between the three types of Atonement-doctrine, surveying them from a number of different angles.

With regard to the structure of the three types, it may be said that the first two may be summarised in the formula which we suggested earlier: the classic type shows a continuity of Divine operation, and a discontinuity in the order of merit and of justice, while the Latin type is opposite to it in both respects. In the classic type the work of Atonement

---

[1] *Cf.* p. 84. It is also true that *Der Mittler* shows in some respects an approach towards the classic idea; but Brunner falls far short of grasping that idea with full clearness.

is accomplished by God Himself in Christ, yet at the same time the passive form also is used: God is reconciled with the world. The alternation is not accidental: He is reconciled only because He Himself reconciles the world with Himself and Himself with the world. The safeguard of the continuity of God's operation is the dualistic outlook, the Divine warfare against the evil that holds mankind in bondage, and the triumph of Christ. But this necessitates a discontinuity of the legal order: there is no satisfaction of God's justice, for the relation of man to God is viewed in the light, not of merit and justice, but of grace.

In the Latin type the legal order is unbroken. Images and analogies are taken continually from the law-courts in the manner dear to the Latin mind. Such analogies can also be used by the classic type; but in the Latin type they dominate the whole conception, and any violation of justice becomes unthinkable. It is at this point, in the payment of the required satisfaction, that the continuity of Divine operation is lost; for the satisfaction is offered by Christ as man, as the sinless Man on behalf of the sinners. At the same time the Atonement is still in some sense the work of God, since He is regarded as planning the Atonement; therefore, also, the doctrine does not require that there is any change in God's attitude to men, even though this may often be taught.

In the third type, the Atonement is no longer regarded as in any true sense carried out by God. Rather, the Reconciliation is the result of some process that takes place in man, such as conversion and amendment. If mention of Christ be made in this connection, His work is no longer thought of as the work of God for man's salvation: He is rather the perfect Example, the Ideal Man, the Head of the race. In so far as Christ's work can affect the relation between God and men, it is chiefly that God now sees mankind in a new light. Therefore in this case, also, it is a matter of an approach of man to God, from below upwards, and not of an approach of God to man.

(ii.) *The Idea of Sin.*—We take next the idea of sin. Here the classic type regards sin as an objective power standing behind men, and the Atonement as the triumph of God over sin, death, and the devil. It might seem, therefore, that this type treats sin as an impersonal force, and so weakens the idea of a direct relationship between God's work and man's soul; for it is over this objective power of evil that God's victory is won. It might seem, too, that the Latin type, which abandons the dualistic outlook and no longer speaks of sin as an objective power, actually gives the idea of a direct and personal relation between God and man, and at the same time a deeper sense of sin; witness Anselm's words, "You have not yet fully weighed the gravity of sin," and his demand that satisfaction for sin must be made to God's justice.

But while there can be no dispute that the Latin doctrine intends to emphasise the gravity of sin, it is another question whether it succeeds in doing so. Our suspicions are aroused by the consideration that the penitential system on the basis of which this doctrine grew up is essentially moralistic, and that mediæval scholasticism never escaped from this moralism. It further becomes evident that at the decisive point the Latin doctrine involves a materialised view of sin; the merits of the satisfaction made by Christ for man's default are treated as transferred or imputed to men. Here, then, plainly, the direct personal relationship between God and the sinner is obscured. Then, too, the very idea of a satisfaction shows that the claim of God on man has not been fully faced. So long as the justice of God can be held to be satisfied by the payment of a compensation for sin, or the endurance of punishment for sin, God's personal demand on man is not adequately expressed, nor is the idea of sin itself seen in its full personal meaning. A comparison with Luther is particularly illuminating. In him we find sin once again treated as an objective power; but at the same time God's claim on man is so spiritually conceived that it cannot be summed up in obedience to any law, and the Latin idea of satisfaction becomes impossible; here, if anywhere, the idea of sin is fully personal. The conclusion, then, is that the view which most fully objectivises sin ends by giving us the deepest and most personal idea of sin.

In the third of the three types it is evident that the idea of sin has become altogether weakened. This is the case not only in the theology of the Enlightenment, which regarded sin as little more than infirmity, but also in Liberal Protestantism generally. The humanistic interpretation of the process of atonement has its ground in the failure of this theology to maintain the radical hostility of God to evil, and His judgment on sin.[2]

But we must pursue the contrast between the classic type and the Latin in regard to the idea of sin. The classic idea

---

[2] The humanistic theology divides man into a 'higher' and a 'lower' nature; in the 'lower' nature it finds the seat of sin, but it regards the 'higher' nature as shading off into the Divine. In contrast with this, the New Testament and Luther agree in finding the root of sin in the centre of man's being, in the egoism of his separate individuality, which makes the advantage or the perfection of the self the aim of human life. In Paul, the contrast between the 'flesh' and the 'spirit' (e.g., Rom. viii. 5 ff.) is not that of man's 'lower' and 'higher' nature; it is the contrast between the self centredness of the natural man, living for himself, doing the desires of the flesh and of the mind, and the new direction which has been given to the lives of those who are under the dominion of the Spirit of God. Similarly, Luther speaks of the natural man as *incurvatus in se;* but faith *rapit nos a nobis et ponit nos extra nos.* And while the Latin type of view regards the Atonement as primarily the remission of the *punishment* of sin, the classic idea directs attention not primarily to the punishment or other consequences of sin, but to the *sin itself.* It is the sin itself that is overcome by Christ, and annihilated; it is from the power of sin itself that man is set free.

has evidently a wider range; for while the Latin doctrine concentrates attention on sin and its accompanying guilt, the classic idea groups sin with a whole series of evil powers—death, the devil, law, the curse. Most constant is the grouping together of sin and death. We have seen how unjustifiable it is to take this thought of deliverance from death as a proof that the whole idea of salvation, according to this view, is merely 'physical' or 'naturalistic.' The real meaning is quite other. If salvation is a deliverance both from sin and from death, and an entrance into life, this of itself forms a safeguard against the degradation either of the idea of sin to a moralistic level, or of the idea of the forgiveness of sin to the level of a mere remission of punishment.

Salvation is therefore regarded positively, not negatively. It is always positive, wherever the classic idea is dominant, whether the actual terms used be the forgiveness of sins, union with God, the deifying of human nature, or some other. On the other hand, with the Latin doctrine the natural tendency is for forgiveness to be regarded negatively; for it is the fruit of the satisfaction made by Christ that the punishment deserved by man is remitted. This contrast makes clear the injustice of the charge made against Luther by Troeltsch and others that his religion consists only in the consolation of the penitent sinner. The fundamental mistake is that the critic has a conception of forgiveness as negative. On the other hand, Luther is always vigorously positive. He never wearies of describing the gift of salvation in whole strings of terms which are more or less synonyms, even to the old patristic language of the 'deification' of human nature. It is, therefore, no accident when, in the Lesser Catechism, he sums up the gift of God as "forgiveness of sins, life, and blessedness"; this is a direct expression of the positive view which is typical of the classic idea of the Atonement. When Christ overcomes the tyrants which hold mankind in bondage, His victory brings with it the Divine blessing, justification, grace, life; the note of triumph rings out.

(iii). *Salvation.*—Our next point is the idea of Salvation, which may be taken as a comprehensive term to describe man's new relation to God. We have already dealt with it in part. The classic idea of salvation is that the victory which Christ gained once for all is continued in the work of the Holy Spirit, and its fruits reaped. So it is in the Fathers, and so it is in Luther; but it is typical of him that the finished work and the continuing work are even more closely connected together than before. The victory of Christ over the powers of evil is an eternal victory, therefore present as well as past. Therefore Justification and Atonement are really one and the same thing; Justification is simply the Atonement brought into the present, so that here and now the Blessing of God prevails over the Curse. It is therefore beside the point to argue whether *Christus pro nobis* or *Christus in nobis* is more emphasised, *propter Christum* or *per Christum*; for these are not two different things, but two sides of the same thing. Both are equally essential.

On the other hand, the Latin doctrine gives us a series of acts standing in a relatively loose connection. The actual atonement consists in the offering of satisfaction by Christ and God's acceptance of it; with this act men have nothing to do except in so far as Christ stands as their representative. Justification is a second act, in which God transfers or imputes to men the merits of Christ; here, again, there is no direct relation between Christ and men. Next, we have Sanctification, a third act with no organic connection with the preceding two.

The 'subjective' type must be seen against the background of the Latin doctrine, as a reaction against it. The observation of the lack of direct relation between Christ and men, which is typical of the Latin doctrine, led to an effort to show along psychological lines what are the features in the portrait of Christ which actually exercise influence upon men. Christ is therefore set forth as the Perfect Example, the Ideal Man, the realisation of human perfection; but the consequence is that the share of God in the process of salvation becomes secondary. What is primary is the change which takes place in men, more or less directly through the influence of Christ. Hence it is not surprising that in Schleiermacher and Ritschl the idea of the Atonement itself moves away from the central place in the scheme, and the word is used to signify the new attitude to the world, characterised by harmony, peace of mind, and self-realisation.

(iv.) *Christ and the Incarnation.*—In our study of the classic idea of the Atonement we have several times noted the close and inseparable connection between the Incarnation and the Atonement; we have seen that this connection is as typical of Luther as of the early church, whose Christological formulæ were developed with the redeeming work of Christ directly in view. The conflict and triumph of Christ is God's own conflict and triumph; it is God who in Christ reconciles the world to Himself. The Incarnation is the necessary presupposition of the Atonement, and the Atonement the completion of the Incarnation.

This does not at all mean that we have here a Docetic Christology, which would do less than justice to the true manhood of Christ; for just as the patristic theology refuses to separate the Son from the Father and make Him an intermediary Being, a δεύτερος Θεός, so it equally refuses to interpret the Incarnation as a Theophany. *His true manhood receives full emphasis.* But yet, again, this does not mean that the redemptive work of Christ is regarded as performed by Him purely as man, or that it gains increased value through the association of the Deity with the Humanity. It is, rather, that Christ is set forth as the Man in whom God

both reveals His essence and carries out His work of deliverance and atonement.

The same intimate connection of Incarnation and Atonement reappears in Luther; only, if possible, the religious
character of the idea is made even clearer, for the very appearance of a naturalistic conception of the Incarnation is
avoided. It is impossible to mistake the meaning for Luther
of the Deity of Christ; the Divine all-mightiness is the only
power that was able to accomplish that which Christ did,
to overcome sin, death, and the curse. The Divine Life, the
Righteousness and the Blessing of God, is present in power,
in 'the despised Man Christ.'

But the Latin type misses this clear conception of the relation between the Incarnation and the Atonement; for God
is no longer the direct agent in the atoning work. Christ as
man makes atonement on man's behalf. The reason is that
the Incarnation was no longer a living doctrine as it had
been in the days of Athanasius; it had become a venerable
inheritance from the past, which must be guarded carefully,
but which was not altogether easy to understand. It is clear
that Anselm's answer to the question, *Cur Deus homo?* is
not so plain and straightforward as that of Irenæus and of
Luther; and the answer of Lutheran Orthodoxy is still less
clear, because of the attempt made to overcome the difficulty of the two natures, which is necessarily involved in
the Latin doctrine.

The 'subjective' type of view may be said to take another
long step on the road on which the Latin doctrine had
entered. That doctrine had laid emphasis on the accomplishment of the atoning work by the human nature of Christ;
the emphasis on the human nature now becomes an exclusive
emphasis, and Christ is treated as simply the Pattern Man.
It is, indeed, important to give these liberal theologians full
credit for their anxiety to maintain the true manhood of

Christ as the historical Jesus; for their Orthodox opponents had often tended to do much less than justice to the true manhood, and in effect to interpret the Incarnation in an almost docetic sense, as a theophany. But this praiseworthy endeavour was only imperfectly carried out; for the Christ presented in their teaching was a peculiarly abstract and unreal Christ, an idealised humanity, and actually became in effect a sort of intermediary between God and mankind. At the same time it is clear that the Incarnation had ceased to take a primary place in their teaching. In the English theologians of this type the Incarnation is interpreted in a semi-Arian rather than in a Nicene sense: it is, rather, that the highest human is the revelation of the Divine, than that God in Christ redeems man. In the Continental liberal theologians, God is at most the ultimate cause of that which Christ does; or, again, through Christ God sees mankind in a new light. In either case the Atonement is not in any true sense the work of God.

(v.) *The Conception of God.*—This brings us to the last point, which is the most fundamental of all: the conception of God. In the classic type of view the idea of God shows a double opposition. The first is, that He is manifested in conflict with evil on the stage of history; here we have a strongly dualistic view. Yet at the same time He is also the all-ruler, the Sovereign; here the dualism is seen not to be ultimate. Second, the Atonement is set forth as the Divine victory over the powers that hold men in bondage. Yet at the same time these very powers are in a measure executants of His own judgment on sin. This opposition reaches its climax in the tension between the Divine Love and the Divine Wrath. But here the solution is not found in any sort of rational settlement; it is rather that the Divine Love prevails over the Wrath, the Blessing overcomes the Curse, by the way of Divine self-oblation and sacrifice. The redeeming work of Christ shows how much the Atonement 'costs' God.

The Latin type has a glimpse of the same opposition, but in a less violent form; for the abstract 'retributive justice' here takes the place of the personal 'wrath,' so that, as it were, God is felt to be more remote. But the solution of the antinomy can fairly be called a rational compromise; for the Justice of God receives a compensation for man's default, so that His Mercy may now be free to act.

In the third type the opposition has disappeared. The intention is to set forth a 'purified,' 'simple' conception of God, whose characteristic is an unchanging Love. But the simplicity is won at the cost of the obscuring of the hostility of the Divine Love to evil; the conception of the Divine Love has become humanised, and at the same time rather obvious and stereotyped.

This brings us back to the first of our five points, the structure of the three types of teaching. The classic type showed us the Atonement as a *movement of God to man*, and God as closely and personally engaged in the work of man's deliverance. In the Latin type God seems to stand more at a distance; for the satisfaction is paid by man, in the person of Christ, to God. In the third type God stands still more at a distance; as far as He is concerned, no atonement is needed, and all the emphasis is on *man's movement to God*, on that which is accomplished in the world of men. That is to say, the essential Christian idea of a way of God to man, which dominates the classic type, is weakened in the Latin type, and lost in the subjective type, in the measure that its leading idea is consistently carried out.

3. THE POSSIBILITY OF A RATIONAL THEORY

I will now add a further comparison of a more formal character. From this point of view we shall see that the classic type stands by itself, in opposition to both the other two. The classic type is characterised by a whole series of contrasts of opposites, which defy rational systematisation, while the other two find rational solutions of the antinomies along theological or psychological lines.

We have had the oppositions of the classic type constantly before us; they have met us at every point, and we have seen that the more fully and deeply the problems are faced, the harder the contradictions become. In Luther we have found them hardest of all. But they are present wherever the classic type appears. God is at once the all-ruler, and engaged in conflict with the powers of evil. These powers are evil powers, and at the same time executants of God's judgment on sin. God is at the same time the Reconciler and the Reconciled. His is the Love and His the Wrath. The Love prevails over the Wrath, and yet Love's condemnation of sin is absolute. The Love is infinite and unfathomable, acting *contra rationem et legem*, justifying men without any satisfaction of the Divine justice or any consideration of human merit; yet at the same time God's claim on men is sharpened to the uttermost.[3]

Every attempt to force this conception into a purely rational scheme is bound to fail; it could only succeed by robbing it of its religious depth. For theology lives and has its being in these combinations of seemingly incompatible opposites. We see in the controversies of the patristic period how the doctrine of the Incarnation and the Redemption

[3] These are not logical contradictions. When, for instance, Luther speaks of the Christian as *simul justus et peccator*, the meaning is not that he is at once and in the same sense sinless and sinful. It is that two different principles are present together in him, so that he can be regarded from two aspects: on the one hand, he is a child of God, alive unto God, justified; on the other, he is not worthy of this Divine vocation. And the more deeply he recognises his Divine vocation, the more he becomes conscious of his own sin: as Luther again says, *Quo quisque magis pius est, eo plus sentit illam pugnam.*

stood as a barrier of rock against the tendencies of the time, which sought to transform theology into a speculative metaphysic or an idealistic philosophy. In Luther the structure of this Christian theology comes out with still greater clearness; at every point Luther's theology is strong in its refusal of a rational scholasticism. For him the God of revelation (*Deus revelatus*) is altogether not to be identified with the God of reason. The point is seen clearest of all when we are shown that *Deus revelatus* is at the same time *Deus absconditus*, who cannot be comprehended in the categories of human thought.

But the Latin doctrine has a wholly different structure. It concentrates its effort upon a rational attempt to explain how the Divine Love and the Divine Justice can be reconciled. The Love of God is regulated by His Justice, and is only free to act within the limits which Justice marks out. *Ratio* and *Lex*, rationality and justice, go hand in hand; but it was just these two which Luther refused to recognise as finally decisive in matters of Christian faith. It is not merely that the scholastic theology is built up on a dialectical and rational basis; it is much more, that in the central questions of Christian faith it allows the dialectical method to have the final say. The attempt is made by the scholastics to elaborate a theology which shall provide a comprehensive explanation of the Divine government of the world, which shall answer all questions and solve all riddles, not only of this world, but also of the world to come.

The humanising theology of Liberal Protestantism, which is the background of the 'subjective' view of the Atonement, stood opposed in many ways to the scholastic theology which it challenged; but it fully accepted the rationalistic ideal. In its treatment of the Atonement it smooths away all the oppositions with which the classic type abounds; all is made rationally clear; even the Love of God becomes rational. Further, it must be observed that this humanising theology is penetrated from end to end by an idealistic philosophy, and seeks to interpret the Christian faith in the light of a monistic and evolutionary world-view. This is no less true of Ritschl and his followers, who make a profession of abjuring metaphysics; for they, too, force theology into the shape of a rational view of the world, which, as the popularity of universalism shows, desires to embrace also the world to come.

These considerations may help to make clear to us one final reason why the classic idea of the Atonement has been suppressed and treated with contempt.[4] When theology sets itself to seek for fully rational explanations of all things, it is only too evident that it must set aside the classic idea, with all its contradictions, as a crude and primitive stage in the attempt to express truth, which is bound to be superseded by more exact and adequate formulations.

Finally, I would call attention to the terminology which I have employed. I have tried to be consistent in speaking of the classic *idea* of the Atonement, never of the, or a, classic *theory*; I have reserved the word *theory*, and usually the word *doctrine*, for the Latin and the 'subjective' types. For the classic idea of the Atonement has never been put forward, like the other two, as a rounded and finished theological *doctrine*; it has always been an idea, a *motif*, a theme, expressed in many different variations. It is not, indeed, that it has lacked clearness of outline; on the contrary, it has been fully definite and unambiguous. But it has never been shaped into a rational theory.

It is therefore of the first importance to distinguish be-

[4] *Cf.* Rashdall, p. 399: "None of them (the schoolmen) blasphemed against God's gift of reason as did Luther. Philosophy and rational theology were things for which Luther frankly confessed that he had no use."

tween the classic idea itself and the forms in which it has
been expressed. Some of the forms in which it has clothed
itself have been the actual provocation and the main cause of
the harsh judgments which have been passed upon it; and,
indeed, when the crude and realistic images which are to be
found in the Fathers and in Luther are interpreted as if they
were seriously intended as theological explanations of the
Atonement, it is only to be expected that they should provoke disgust. But that is to miss the point. The images are
but popular helps for the understanding of the idea. It is the
idea itself that is primary.

*   *   *   *   *

My aim in this book has been throughout an historical, not
an apologetic aim. It has been my endeavour to make clear,
to the best of my power, the nature of the various types of
teaching on the subject of the Atonement as they have
emerged in history. In particular, I have tried to fix the actual character of that type of teaching which I have called
the classic idea, because it has been so grievously misinterpreted and neglected; and I have tried to show how important is the place which it has actually held in the history of
Christian thought. I have not had any intention of writing
an *apologia* for the classic idea; and if my exposition has
shaped itself into something like a vindication of it, I would
plead that it is because the facts themselves point that way.
For it can scarcely be denied that the classic idea emerged
with Christianity itself, and on that ground alone cannot be
refused a claim such as neither the Latin nor the subjective
type of teaching can make, to embody that which is most
genuinely Christian.

Let it be added, in conclusion, that if the classic idea of
the Atonement ever again resumes a leading place in Christian theology, it is not likely that it will revert to precisely

the same forms of expression that it has used in the past; its revival will not consist in a putting back of the clock. It is the idea itself that will be essentially the same: the fundamental idea that the Atonement is, above all, a movement of God to man, not in the first place a movement of man to God. We shall hear again its tremendous paradoxes: that God, the all-ruler, the Infinite, yet accepts the lowliness of the Incarnation; we shall hear again the old realistic message of the conflict of God with the dark, hostile forces of evil, and His victory over them by the Divine self-sacrifice; above all, we shall hear again the note of triumph.

For my own part, I am persuaded that no form of Christian teaching has any future before it except such as can keep steadily in view the reality of the evil in the world, and go to meet the evil with a battle-song of triumph. Therefore I believe that the classic idea of the Atonement and of Christianity is coming back—that is to say, the genuine, authentic Christian faith.

INDEX

(See also the Summary of the Argument, p. xiii)